Praise for *The Age of Promise*

"Randy gives us an in-depth look at the promises of God and shows us how we can walk in freedom and victory in every area of our lives. Filled with personal stories and biblical truths, I know this book will give you hope and help you grow in your walk with the Lord."

—Robert Morris, founding senior pastor of Gateway
Church and bestselling author of *The Blessed
Life*, *The God I Never Knew*, and *Frequency*

"Randy Robison is a gifted writer and thinker who helps us examine the scriptures and our callings in a fresh way. You'll love what you find in these pages."

—Margaret Feinberg, author of *Flourish*

"Randy Robison is passionate about the word of God. He loves to dig deep and search for truth. I believe that as you read this book, the promises from God's word will grow your faith, hope, and confidence in who God is and what he says!"

—John Bevere, bestselling author and
cofounder of Messenger International

THE
AGE
—— OF ——
PROMISE

THE
AGE
—— OF ——
PROMISE

Escape *the* Shadows
of the Law *to*
Live *in the* Light *of* Christ

RANDY
ROBISON

NELSON
BOOKS

An Imprint of Thomas Nelson

Published in Nashville, Tennessee, by Nelson Books, an imprint of Thomas Nelson. Nelson Books and Thomas Nelson are registered trademarks of HarperCollins Christian Publishing, Inc.

Thomas Nelson titles may be purchased in bulk for educational, business, fund-raising, or sales promotional use. For information, please e-mail SpecialMarkets@ThomasNelson.com.

Any Internet addresses, phone numbers, or company or product information printed in this book are offered as a resource and are not intended in any way to be or to imply an endorsement by Thomas Nelson, nor does Thomas Nelson vouch for the existence, content, or services of these sites, phone numbers, companies, or products beyond the life of this book.

Unless otherwise noted, Scripture quotations are taken from New American Standard Bible.® Copyright © 1960, 1962, 1963, 1968, 1971, 1972, 1973, 1975, 1977, 1995 by The Lockman Foundation. Used by permission. (www. Lockman.org)

Scripture quotations marked NIV are taken from the Holy Bible, New International Version®, NIV®. Copyright © 1973, 1978, 1984, 2011 by Biblica, Inc.™ Used by permission of Zondervan. All rights reserved worldwide. www. zondervan.com. The "NIV" and "New International Version" are trademarks registered in the United States Patent and Trademark Office by Biblica, Inc.™

Scripture quotations marked KJV are taken from the King James Version.

ISBN 978-1-4002-07541 (eBook)

Library of Congress Cataloging-in-Publication Data

ISBN 978-1-4002-07534
Library of Congress Control Number: 2017958466

Printed in the United States of America

18 19 20 21 22 LSC 6 5 4 3 2 1

Contents

Introduction

The End Is Here

The end of all things is near.
1 PETER 4:7

The end can be frightening. The end of a relationship, the end of a job, the end of life—endings usually hold uncertainty, despair, and pain. And yet they can also be liberating when they signify the completion of something that allows us to move on to something better.

Our New Testament was written in a time of completion. It came about when the old covenant God had made with the people of Israel was fulfilled in Christ. The shadows in which the Israelites walked—ancient prophecies yet to come to fruition, mysteries not quite understood, promises yet to be realized—were all illuminated and fulfilled by the arrival of God's Son. And with the ending of that old covenant came a beginning when God established a new covenant with all people. All of creation passed from one era to another. It was a time of transition, anticipated for centuries and expressed throughout the universe.

Everything up to that point, from Adam and Eve's expulsion from the garden of Eden to the angel's proclamation to Mary and Joseph, had laid the foundation for God's intricate plan to bring salvation to all of mankind. The culmination of that divine design was Jesus Christ. His birth, life, death, and resurrection changed everything. The generation that witnessed these events was the last of its kind. When the final person born of the previous age breathed his or her last breath, the old era ended and the new Christ-initiated era came into its fullness.

On the cusp of that day, as the old came to a close and the new ignited an explosion felt across the earth, the apostle Peter penned three words—*Telos pas eggizo*—a noun, adjective, and verb, which we translate as "the end of all things is near." *Telos* signifies the last in a series, a close, and a purpose. *Pas* ties it all together, everything and everyone. *Eggizo* indicates a fast approach, joining one thing to another. According to Peter, everything significant in the eyes of God was coming together with the purpose of ushering in a new era.

To the believers spread across Asia Minor, as Nero persecuted Christians in a reign of terror and abomination, Peter proclaimed the fast arrival of a series of events that would impact everyone and bring the existing age to a close. Christ's predictions on the Mount of Olives were about to come true. The temple in Jerusalem would soon be destroyed, and Jesus' prophecies would be fulfilled.

In the dusk of the old age, a new era was rising. One based not on the law, but on grace. One based not on the works of man, but on the works of Christ. The principles of this emerging age had been foreshadowed throughout the Old Testament, and now they were becoming reality.

This is the era in which we live today. Christ has been revealed. Truth has been proclaimed. The curse has been broken. Satan has been defeated. You and I are blessed to live in this period. It is a time of victory, a time when the principles formed in the Old Testament have been transformed in Christ. When we understand the implications of all that Jesus has done and apply these ancient principles made new, our lives change in this world. We learn how to think, speak, and act each day, and are preserved for all of eternity. God's Word is a lamp to our feet and light to our path guiding our daily steps (Ps. 119:105). Through it we can truly live lives of victory, because we live in an age of promise.

CHAPTER 1

The Promise of Deliverance

Many are the afflictions of the righteous,
*But the L*ORD *delivers him out of them all.*

PSALM 34:19

As I walked into the brothel in southeast Asia, accompanied by a missions team equipped with hidden cameras and microphones, I couldn't help but think, *If my daughter was in here, I'd do anything to get her out.* Images of Liam Neeson in *Taken* flashed through my mind, and I saw myself blasting through armies of bad guys as these young girls cowered behind me, desperate for freedom. But reality wasn't anything like that.

There were no locks on the outsides of the doors, no cages, no Mafia types around. In fact, we didn't see a single man. It was a dumpy motel with older women cooking food and managing the girls. We sat in a karaoke room as they served warm beer we didn't drink and snacks we eyed with suspicion. I sipped a Diet Coke, sang an

American rock song on the karaoke machine, and talked to a couple of girls. After we determined they were all adults and seemed to be there of their own volition, we said subtle prayers for them, left a large tip, and politely excused ourselves, much to their dismay.

It was not quite what we expected when we went into that small town to explore potential ministry opportunities for Rescue LIFE, our ministry's program to end sex trafficking. Even so, we all recognized the great need that exists in all such places: deliverance.

Since the fall of mankind, we have all needed deliverance. Each person's individual smallness in a vast universe demands something or someone bigger to step in and take the reins. We need protection from natural disasters, human evil, and the spiritual Enemy who seeks to steal, kill, and destroy. And you know what? God promises us that deliverance in the Bible.

The concept of deliverance appears throughout Scripture in several forms. Jacob's first prayer for deliverance from the hand of his brother, Esau, was one seeking rescue. He pleaded with God to rescue him from one who had evil intentions toward him. This need for rescue was repeated throughout the Old Testament. David prayed to be delivered from King Saul, who sought to kill him. Those pilgrims following Ezra to Jerusalem were delivered from ambush. The Israelites' history is one story after another of God delivering them from foreign armies.

Another catalyst of God's deliverance was the need for escape. Jacob and his sons escaped the famine in Canaan because of Joseph's wisdom and authority in Egypt. When the Israelites rebelled against God under the reign of King Rehoboam and King Shishak's Egyptian army came to destroy them, they humbled themselves before God and escaped death, although God allowed them to become slaves. In Joel's vision of the coming judgment on the "day of the LORD," he foresaw the destruction of Jerusalem in AD 70 but noted that "whoever calls on the name of the LORD / Will be delivered; / For on Mount Zion and in Jerusalem / There will be those who escape" (Joel 2:32). Those who heeded the warnings of Joel to flee Judea into the mountains when certain signs appeared escaped that awful judgment and death. Whether we find ourselves in the middle of a bad situation or we escape the situation altogether, God is our deliverer.

The New Testament introduced deliverance as a response to the need for healing. The hemorrhaging woman who touched Jesus' garment was delivered from her illness. The lame beggar at the Beautiful Gate was delivered from his disability when Peter and John spoke to him in Christ's name. James wrote that believers should pray for the sick so that they would be delivered from their sickness and "made well." Deliverance from disease can be part of God's overall plan to make us spiritually whole.

The last function of deliverance is addressing the need for salvation. This type of deliverance is what the psalmist wrote about and what Paul knew was coming when he was in prison facing possible execution. This is the ultimate deliverance from the evils of this world; resting in this inevitable future enables us to remain strong in our faith regardless of the earthly outcome of our difficult situations. The worst that can happen is death, which leads to eternal life in a glorious heaven.

Maintaining an eternal view of creation gives us hope during the hardships of our lives, but I want to focus on how deliverance relates to the trials of this life, the promises given in Scripture, and the expectations we can have as we journey through this temporal place.

Deliver Us from Evil

When Jesus asked his Father to "deliver us from evil" as he modeled prayer (Matt. 6:13), Jesus highlighted deliverance. The Greek word we translate *deliver* has two meanings: "rescue" and "God drawing us to himself."[1]

The concept of being rescued needs little explanation. There is evil in the world that God can keep us safe from, so we ask that of him. This encompasses deliverance from the physical threats of this world as well as deliverance through Christ from spiritual threats. The same Greek word in Christ's prayer is employed in Paul's declaration: "For He rescued us from the domain of darkness, and transferred us to the kingdom of His beloved Son, in whom we have redemption, the forgiveness of sins" (Col. 1:13–14).

The other meaning of *rhoumai*, the Greek word for deliverance, is not used as commonly in Scripture, but it expresses a remarkable truth. Our deliverance, whether physical or not, is directly tied to God drawing us to himself. When Paul wrote to the church in Thessalonica, he warned them about what would soon happen to them, paralleling Christ's warnings of their tribulation. But he also wrote that before it happened, there would be deliverance for followers of Christ because God would draw them to himself and thus take them out of harm's way (1 Thess. 1:10).

Though the vast majority of us have never faced the persecution the first-century church did, I can't help but wonder how many of our personal tragedies, failures, and hardships could be avoided if we simply drew closer to God. I know I could have avoided a few! Peter noted that "the Lord knows how to rescue the godly from temptation" (2 Peter 2:9). We need not fear temptation if we're walking closely with the One called *Jehovah Mephalti*—the Lord my Deliverer. It is common for us to wait until we are in dire need of rescue to cry out to God, but rescue is already here if we will just stay close to Christ. When we do so, we hear more clearly his direction for each step along the way and can steer clear of unnecessary problems we are prone to create in our shortsightedness.

Sometimes, though, God has a plan for our hardships. In another letter Paul wrote, he remarked to Timothy, "What persecutions I endured, and out of them all the Lord rescued me!" (2 Tim. 3:11). Note that Paul didn't say he was rescued from persecution, but rather he endured persecution and *then* the Lord rescued him. Of course, we all want to be delivered from problems, but I dare say it's more common for us to be delivered *through* our difficult situations.

James wrote, "Consider it all joy, my brethren, when you encounter various trials, knowing that the testing of your faith produces endurance. And let endurance have its perfect result, so that you may be perfect and complete, lacking in nothing" (James 1:2–4). If God hasn't delivered you *from* something, it's most likely because he wants to deliver you *through* it, in order to build endurance and make you whole.

Endurance is a tool God uses for our growth. When Jesus warned his disciples of the coming tribulation and destruction of Jerusalem, he said, "By your endurance you will gain your lives" (Luke 21:19). (The word for *lives* is sometimes translated as "souls.") As a coach pushes his players through tough workouts so that they can perform better in competition, God allows us to go through difficulty to build us up, not tear us down. This perspective offers hope and confidence, and once we understand this, we will discover joy in the process.

Keys to Deliverance

God is our deliverer, but does that require anything of us? Absolutely. The story of the Israelites' deliverance from slavery in Egypt described what we must do today to take hold of our own promised deliverance.

Their journey foreshadowed the mental, emotional, spiritual, and (in some cases) physical journeys we must take. As we explore the story, we'll find key steps of obedience we should incorporate into our own lives, as well as numerous principles that are as true today as they were thousands of years ago.

Let's start with the story of Moses, as told in the book of Exodus. After Joseph rescued his family from famine and they had relocated from Canaan to Egypt, the tribes "were fruitful and increased greatly, and multiplied, and became exceedingly mighty" (Ex. 1:7). This eventually caused problems for the Egyptians. A new king rose up—one who did not know Joseph—and he feared the Israelites, even though they presented no threat. He began oppressing them. He made them slaves. Then he ordered all newborn males to be killed on the spot. When the Hebrew midwives skirted that command, the cruel king commanded all infant males be thrown into the Nile River. Against this backdrop, God delivered one infant from the river, placing him in the king's court. His name was Moses.

Moses grew up as an adopted son to the pharaoh, but as he got older, he began to notice the suffering of his people. When he came upon an Egyptian savagely beating an Israelite, Moses killed him and then fled east across the Sinai Peninsula to the land of the Midianites. He eventually found a wife there, and she bore him a son. Meanwhile, back in Egypt the Israelites continued to suffer. God appeared to Moses and said, "I have surely seen the affliction of My people who are in Egypt, and have given heed to their cry because of their taskmasters, for I am aware of their sufferings" (Ex. 3:7).

This is the first truth we need to know about suffering: God sees it. He is aware. "Are not five sparrows sold for two cents?" Jesus asked. "Yet not one of them is forgotten before God. Indeed, the very hairs of your head are all numbered. Do not fear; you are more valuable than many sparrows" (Luke 12:6–7). Suffering can bring a sense of isolation and make us begin to think we are alone in our troubles, but we are not forgotten. Our Deliverer knows, and he is able to change the landscape of the world to rescue us.

God called Moses to deliver his people out of bondage. He said, "I have come down to deliver them from the power of the Egyptians, and to bring them up from that land to a good and spacious land, to a land flowing with milk and honey" (Ex. 3:8). That's the second truth we must understand: he wants to deliver us. And not just from one bad situation to a less miserable one, but to a place of fulfillment and fruitfulness.

We are not supposed to live in bondage. Paul wrote, "It was for freedom that Christ set us free" (Gal. 5:1). If you have been convinced that freedom is unattainable, then you have bought into a lie. When you give yourself willingly as a servant of God, he does not want you under the rule of anyone or anything else. And though we offer ourselves as servants, he raises us up as his sons and daughters, making us heirs to his kingdom. We are meant to be free.

When Moses received the call from God to bring this freedom to his people, he hesitated. He knew he wasn't qualified, capable, or worthy to be such a leader on his own. In fact, he wasn't even looking to rescue the Israelites when God called him. He was "pasturing the flock" of his father-in-law when he noticed the burning bush that wasn't burning up and thought, *That's weird.* He was minding his own business when God dropped in on him and called him to one of the greatest roles in human history. Moses' response was as human as it gets: "Who am I to do that?" But with God's promise to be with him, Moses had hope, because he understood that he simply had to be obedient and allow God to make it happen. That's the next principle: God delivers out of his goodness, not because of our abilities or merits. Paul wrote, "For by grace you have been saved through faith; and that not of yourselves, it is the gift of God; not as a result of works, so that no one may boast" (Eph. 2:8–9).

Deliverance is usually beyond our capabilities. Sometimes our problems are a result of our own faults. If we think we can deliver ourselves, then we're doomed to fail. We have to humble ourselves and say, "Deliver us from evil," as Jesus instructed us to pray, because deliverance is beyond our grasp. Our hope lies in the fact that it is never beyond God's. In our weakness, he is strong.

With God strengthening him, Moses went to Pharaoh and demanded the release of the Israelites. Of course Pharaoh refused, so God unleashed a series of plagues on the Egyptians, forcing that mighty empire to beg the Israelites to leave in the end. God's people walked away from their lives of slavery with their heads held high. And that's the first step of obedience you and I must take to obtain the promise of deliverance: walk away from what has been holding us captive.

How often do we stay in bondage simply because we don't walk away? Granted, there are things we can't escape that easily. If you're battling health issues, it's not so simple. But many of our prisons have open doors if we'll just choose to leave. With God's power, we can walk away from anger, bitterness, unforgiveness, strife, jealousy, and so many other shackles. We can leave bad habits behind by staying away from places that draw us in, cutting off avenues of temptation and sin, and removing ourselves from situations that do nothing but keep us bound. If you're waiting for deliverance, take a good hard look at whether or not you need to simply walk away from your Egypt. You may not know exactly where you're going, but if you can get out, do so quickly and leave behind everything that enslaves you.

After the Israelites left Egypt, Pharaoh did a really dumb thing.

He changed his mind and sent his armies after them. Frankly, I've never understood this. He had just been brought to his knees for his defiance of God. He had seen inexplicable natural disasters. His people had suffered like never before. His own firstborn son died, along with the firstborn of everyone who wasn't covered by the blood of the sacrificial lambs. And Pharaoh hadn't simply let the Israelites go. He had said, "Go, and bless me also" (Ex. 12:32). He'd actually asked for their blessing, and then he tried to kill them!

Of course, that didn't go so well for him. His armies drowned in the Red Sea. But in that there's another lesson for us today. When we walk away from bondage, it may pursue us. That addiction may try to overtake you again. Your thoughts may return to that thing that's held you. But keep going. Sins are doomed to be destroyed. Continue moving in the right direction. Even if an endless sea seems to stand in your way, go with God. He'll part that sea and use it to swallow up your enemies.

Once safely away from their captors, the Israelites began their journey to the promised land. It was not right next door to their land of captivity, so they had to start walking, as is typically the case with us. Sometimes God does deliver us from things instantly, as when Jesus healed people or when an earthquake opened the prison doors for Paul and Silas, but most of the time it's a journey. Reaching our own "promised lands" requires time, effort, and a constant pursuit of God. Such was the case with the Israelites. Before long, they were complaining: "Would that we had died by the LORD's hand in the land of Egypt, when we sat by the pots of meat, when we ate bread to the full; for you have brought us out into this wilderness to kill this whole assembly with hunger" (Ex. 16:3).

When I read that, I think, *Seriously? You'd rather have been struck down by God than be free? I know the desert is a rough place to live, but at least you're alive!* Truth be told, captivity can sometimes bring a perverse form of satisfaction. Live Free or Die makes a fine state motto, but when put to the test, many people would rather live bound than face suffering. The Israelites demonstrated this kind of thinking and an astonishing lack of faith. They had seen the plagues, been rescued from generations of slavery, and watched the mightiest army in their known world drown in a nature-defying phenomenon. But in their shortsightedness, all they knew was that they were hungry—hungrier than they had been when they were slaves. They were petulant children, but that didn't change God. He was still a good Father.

Moses told Aaron to tell the people, "Come near before the LORD, for He has heard your grumblings" (Ex. 16:9). That's quite the response. As a father of four, I have definitely experienced times when one or more of my children was grumbling, and my typical response was not "Come sit by Daddy." Unless, perhaps, I was about to chastise them. But that's not what God did. He basically said, "I hear you griping, and now I'm going to bless you." He sent manna and quail—bread in the morning, meat in the evening.

When we walk away from bondage, especially one that has a perverse sense of comfort, it's easy to feel dissatisfied or empty in the aftermath. Ask anyone who used to smoke a pack a day. Or someone who broke up with a boyfriend because she knew the relationship wasn't right. Walking away can leave a hole, and we feel the lack of what was once there. It's easy to complain. And when we feel grumpy or irritable, the natural instinct is to take the further step of thinking that God must not want much to do with us. But again we see both facets of deliverance—his rescue and his desire to draw us to himself—in his response to "come near." He hears us. He knows. And he's eager to fill us.

This brings us to the next key of deliverance: we must be filled with the Holy Spirit. That means continually pursuing God's truth, power, and presence. When the Israelites first left Egypt, God led them from place to place with a pillar of cloud by day and a pillar of fire by night. When God delivers you, you must keep pursuing him. "Be filled with the Spirit," Paul wrote (Eph. 5:18). Don't leave any room for the Enemy to return once you've been freed.

Jesus warned us about this when he spoke to the religious Jews who rejected him:

> "Now when the unclean spirit goes out of a man, it passes through waterless places seeking rest, and does not find it. Then it says, 'I will return to my house from which I came'; and when it comes, it finds it unoccupied, swept, and put in order. Then it goes and takes along with it seven other spirits more wicked than itself, and they go in and live there; and the last state of that man becomes worse than the first. That is the way it will also be with this evil generation." (Matt. 12:43–45)

If we don't let God fill us as we pursue him, then we inadvertently leave room for the Enemy to come back in. We must fill ourselves with God day by day. The Israelites' provisions in the desert were good for only one day, except on the sixth day when God allowed it to carry them through the Sabbath. It's the same for us. Jesus told us to pray, "Give us this day our daily bread" (Matt. 6:11). That's not just a suggestion; it's a promise of daily fulfillment and a reminder of the fact that we need to be filled every day.

Finally, along our path of deliverance, we need to be prepared to fight. Deliverance is not passive on our part; it's active. It wasn't long before the Israelites were attacked in the desert. The Amalekites came after them, and they had to fight. God was with them and they won, but there would be more battles on their way to their promised land. Just as Paul was delivered *through* the tribulation (2 Tim. 4:17), the Israelites were not delivered from the fight altogether. Rather, they were guaranteed victory as they continued on the journey.

God told them, "I will be an enemy to your enemies and an adversary to your adversaries. . . . I will drive them out before you little by little, until you become fruitful and take possession of the land" (Ex. 23:22, 30). Notice two important points in these promises: First, God will fight for you. He's on your side. If he declared himself an enemy to the enemies of those bound to the old covenant, how much more is he on the side of those covered under the new covenant with his Son! Second, God said the promised land would be taken "little by little." Again, we see an ongoing struggle with a guaranteed outcome. There are many destructive things in our lives that take time to eradicate. The lesson from the Israelites is to keep fighting and anticipate the inevitable victory.

Even If . . .

In an honest discussion about deliverance, we must address those situations when deliverance doesn't seem to come. John the Baptist was beheaded. Stephen was stoned to death. Peter and Paul were both executed by Nero in Rome. If deliverance means always escaping death, then the concept is all an illusion. Last time I checked, nobody leaves this earth alive.

Paul obviously understood this as he wrote to the church in Philippi from a Roman prison: "I know that this will turn out for my deliverance" (Phil. 1:19). Did he believe that he would be freed and live a life of longevity? Certainly not. He followed that by saying,

"Christ will even now, as always, be exalted in my body, whether by life or by death" (Phil. 1:20).

For Paul and for all of us, deliverance allows us to live lives that glorify Christ no matter the circumstances. Paul concerned himself only with the desire to shamelessly proclaim Christ and honor him as long as he lived. Immediately after that declaration, he wrote these often-quoted words: "For to me, to live is Christ and to die is gain" (Phil. 1:21). If death is gain for those in Christ, then we can be delivered *from* death or delivered *through* death. It's the ultimate win-win scenario. We are delivered either way.

The right attitude toward physical deliverance from evil can be found in Daniel 3. You probably know the story. Shadrach, Meshach, and Abed-nego were Jewish leaders who had been appointed to govern the province of Babylon, which was part of the Babylonian Empire under the rule of Nebuchadnezzar. Nebuchadnezzar had commissioned a ninety-foot statue and then held a public dedication ceremony. In advance, he had sent out an edict that ordered everyone to bow to the statue when the band played. The three Jewish leaders did not bow. Some Chaldeans ratted them out, and Shadrach, Meshach, and Abed-nego were brought before a very unhappy Nebuchadnezzar. In his magnanimity, he granted them a second chance to bow down. If they still would not, then they would be thrown into a fire pit. They refused, so he threw them in. But, inexplicably, they didn't burn, and a fourth man was even seen in the fire with them. Seeing this unexplainable phenomenon, Nebuchadnezzar had a quasi-conversion in the sense that he freed them and ordered none to speak ill of their God. (If anyone did, he ordered them to be "torn limb from limb and their houses reduced to a rubbish heap" [Dan. 3:29]. He had the fear of God but largely missed the spirit of the whole thing.)

The part I want you to hear in this story is Shadrach, Meshach, and Abed-nego's response to Nebuchadnezzar's threat to kill them. It shows us exactly how we should look at physical deliverance from the dangers of this world, including death. They said, "Our God whom we serve is able to deliver us from the furnace of blazing fire; and He will deliver us out of your hand, O king. But even if He does not, let it be known to you, O king, that we are not going to serve your gods or worship the golden image that you have set up" (Dan. 3:17–18).

When facing death, they declared three things. First, they said, "God is able." Never doubt it. He can strike your enemies down, cause an earthquake to set you free, or rain down hailstones on your persecutors. He created heaven and earth, and he can move them to get you out of danger.

Second, they said, "He will." Maybe God had revealed to them how their particular situation would unfold, or maybe they were just optimistic. We don't really know. But when people have the opposite attitude—"God can help me, but I bet he won't"—that pretty much tells you where they are on the faith meter. Instead, let's choose to walk in faith. It's not self-delusional to say, "I'm choosing to believe God will rescue me." It's right to expect the best. We should approach every situation with hope, not despair.

Third, they said, "But even if He does not." This is where the real measure of faith lies. It takes faith to say, "God can." It takes even more to say, "God will." But it takes a boatload of faith to say, "But even if he doesn't." You can only say that if you have an eternal perspective, a to-live-is-Christ-and-to-die-is-gain attitude. It's a beautiful stubbornness that declares God's rule regardless of the outcome.

The promise of deliverance is not the promise to escape death. Instead, it is the promise that one day we will leave this temporal, tainted world to live eternally in God's presence, and until then we are free and strengthened to live in a way that glorifies Christ. No matter how difficult, painful, and tragic this life may be, it ends extremely well. There is a place where all enemies are defeated and there is eternal peace and freedom, and it's reserved for believers. When we escape earthly dangers, we win. And when we escape this earth for good, we win even more.

How Long? (To Sing This Song)

Often when we're in the middle of life's difficulties, we cannot see the purposes of God for some time. We cannot see how God will deliver us. When David was in a time of trouble, he asked, "How long?" He pleaded with God, "Return, O LORD, rescue my soul; / Save me because of Your lovingkindness" (Ps. 6:3–4). When Paul wrote that "God causes all things to work together for good to those who love God" (Rom. 8:28), he didn't say, "God causes all things to be good," or "All things are good." Let's be honest: Some things really suck. Relationships can be tumultuous. Working to provide for your family can be difficult. Divorce is usually painful. Disease is always miserable. War is hell. Death is loss. Some things are bad and always will be. The promise Paul wrote about is that God can take the bad and make something good on the other side of it.

I recently had the privilege of interviewing Victoria Arlen, an amazing young woman with an astonishing story. At age eleven, she started experiencing flu-like symptoms. Within two weeks, she slipped into a vegetative state, completely unable to speak, eat, or move. When she was diagnosed with two rare conditions that attack the nerves in the spine, doctors gave up on her. Perhaps most horrifying is the fact that she was aware of everything happening to her. She was held hostage in a body that wouldn't respond, but her mind and spirit were sharp.

Victoria told me that it was during this time that she grew close to God. She begged him to set her free from the paralysis, and after nearly four years, her deliverance began. She made eye contact with her mother, who asked her to blink if she could hear her. Victoria blinked as frantically as she could. Progress continued slowly as she learned to wiggle her fingers, straighten her arms, and finally regain the ability to speak and move. Still, she was paralyzed from the waist down. Her response was to take to the water, where she swam using just her arms. In 2012, she competed in the Paralympic Games in London. She took home three silver medals and a gold. In 2015, she became a commentator for ESPN, covering the Summer and Winter X Games and reporting for *SportsCenter*. And in 2016, she walked unassisted and without any noticeable difficulty into our studios for the *LIFE Today* television program.

Why did God allow her to experience something straight out of a Hollywood horror movie? Why did she have to work so hard for incremental healing? I have no idea. But I could see the good on the other side of it. Eleven years after a mysterious illness sent a little girl to the hospital for the start of a nightmarish journey, I saw a beautiful witness forged in the fires of adversity.

Lack of understanding and clarity in the midst of a trial is not uncommon. Consider Joseph. He was sold into slavery by his brothers, falsely accused while faithfully serving his master, and unjustly confined to prison. There had to be days, weeks, and months when he wondered if his childhood dreams had been completely derailed. But eventually he was put in a position of power, even though it was in the land of his captors. When famine struck Egypt and the surrounding regions, as God had shown him in a dream, Joseph was prepared. When his brothers—the ones who had sold him into slavery decades earlier—came to him seeking help, he made this statement: "God sent me before you to preserve for you a remnant in the earth, and to keep you alive by a great deliverance" (Gen. 45:7).

God had prepared him, forged him in the fires of adversity, to fulfill a purpose. Joseph became an agent of deliverance, though he couldn't begin to see that when he was in the midst of his troubles. And eventually God gave him the greatest privilege. From Joseph and his brothers came the twelve tribes of Israel and, ultimately, Jesus, the savior of the world.

Help Wanted

In addition to the promise of God's deliverance, I believe there is another promise in this age of Christ. It is revealed in an often-overlooked story in 2 Kings 13. After Israel divided into two kingdoms (Israel in the north, Judah in the south), the Northern Kingdom was ruled by nineteen kings, each one often worse than his predecessor. Right in the middle of their estimated 212-year dynasty, Jehoahaz ruled for seventeen years. As those before him had done, he encouraged the people to worship at temples other than God's true temple in Jerusalem, which the first king, Jeroboam, had created. So God allowed an enemy, King Hazael of Aram, to oppress them.

Here's the scenario: A bad ruler encouraged ungodly behavior, people followed, and things got bad. In the middle of this self-imposed need for deliverance, King Jehoahaz asked God for help. Keep in mind, this was a rotten king. He openly encouraged pagan styles of worship, which is right there at number two on the Ten Commandments carved in stone. He only went to God because his back was against the wall. But you know what? God knew what his children were going through, he loved his people, and he answered the wicked king's prayer.

The passage simply says, "The LORD gave Israel a deliverer, so that they escaped from under the hand of the Arameans; and the sons of Israel lived in their tents as formerly" (2 Kings 13:5). Rebellious people asked God for help, he came through for them, and things went back to normal. These were not righteous, obedient, God-fearing people. Sure, they were part of God's chosen people, but they were seriously prodigal, especially the king. Even so, God answered their pleas for deliverance.

If you think you have to clean up, get right, or make yourself good enough for God before asking for his help, then you've got it backward. It's right there in the mess—including the one you've made—that God wants you to turn to him and ask for help. And it's into your mess that he sends a deliverer.

Mini-sermon aside, here's why I mention this story: God is the deliverer at the end of the day—you know that by now—but it says in the passage that he "gave Israel a deliverer," meaning he used someone or something to deliver them. Maybe it was a hailstorm raining down on the armies of Aram, but if I had to guess, I'd bet it was a person, a fighter with a quick sword, a sharp mind, and endless courage. We don't know for sure because the Scriptures don't tell us exactly what or who that was. But the point is that God can use people as instruments of his deliverance. He did it with Joseph. He did it with David. In fact, he did it a lot.

In this age of Christendom, God is looking for a different kind of fighter, one with the sword of his Spirit, the mind of Christ, and the courage to lead the battle. We are called to be agents of deliverance. That may mean sharing the gospel for the salvation of others. It may mean making people well through diet, fitness, or medicine. It may mean healing hearts and minds through counseling, discipleship, and prayer. It may mean adopting unwanted children or rescuing victims of human trafficking. How it looks for you depends on what God asks you to do. If you want to know how you are to be an agent of deliverance, don't ask me or anyone else. Ask God! He will answer, and then he will empower you to do whatever you are called to do.

When Jesus first sent the twelve apostles out to share what he had taught them, he told them, among other things, to "heal the sick, raise the dead, cleanse the lepers, cast out demons" (Matt. 10:8). As much as I think I would have some serious fun doing those things, God has not empowered me to do any of them, so that's not my lane to be running in. (At least not yet. I'm open to any of them at any time!) I do believe, however, that God has enabled me to search for truth, understand his Word, and share it with others. If I can write anything that helps God draw someone to him, then I am being an agent of deliverance.

Isaiah prophesied, "A Redeemer will come to Zion, / And to those who turn from transgression in Jacob" (Isa. 59:20). That Redeemer is Jesus Christ only. His fulfillment of the old covenant completed the transformation into the new one, where he and he alone reigns. There will never be another Messiah, and our deliverance will never be through the power of anyone other than Christ. However, we can be used by God for his purpose. In fact, we are supposed to be just that.

Living the Promise

As you walk confidently in the promise of deliverance, remember your position as a child of God. Trust him in every situation for deliverance, whether it comes immediately, incrementally, or eternally. Look for opportunities to rescue others from distress. When you walk in the unique power God gives you in order to advance his kingdom, you point others to the Deliverer. So take God up on his offer to deliver you, and go be his agent of deliverance for someone else.

CHAPTER 2

The Promise of Sacrifice

He has been manifested to put away
sin by the sacrifice of Himself.
HEBREWS 9:26

Between my junior and senior years of college, I had the opportunity to spend a week in Europe running audio and video for the *LIFE Today* television program. We visited an AIDS orphanage in Romania, ministered in East Germany before the Berlin Wall fell, and preached in Poland. After our assignment was complete, I stayed on an extra week with another guy my age, and we hopped the Eurorail with no particular destination in mind.

Eventually we decided to check out the Hohensalzburg Fortress in Austria, the largest fully preserved castle in central Europe. Built in 1077, it sits high on the Mönchsberg, a steep hill that towers above Salzburg. I couldn't tell you how to get there, because we got lost walking on a narrow road at the base of it and decided to cut through the woods rather than wind around the mountain. Our off-the-beaten-path route was steep—so steep that we had to hold on to small trees as we climbed up—but it wasn't that far of a distance. We could see a wall of the fortress at the top of the hill through the trees. We had found a shortcut!

Once we made it there, we climbed two walls and somehow ended up on a rampart that led to the upper areas of the castle. There we ran into other tourists and blended in with the crowd to see the sights. When we exited out the front, though, I glanced back and saw the entrance. There was a ticket window.

"I think we were supposed to pay," I said. (I couldn't really read the sign since my German is *nicht gut*.)

My friend looked back and started laughing.

We kept walking. We didn't mean to be in the wrong, but we were. To make it worse, when we realized we were in the wrong, we didn't make it right. To this day, we still owe the Austrian people a few Schillings.

We all make mistakes, whether by simply missing the mark or purposely doing something we know to be wrong. Failure is a part of life, even for believers. In the Hohensalzburg Fortress of life, we have all been caught trespassing, and the ticket price is way beyond our ability to pay. Attempting to self-atone for these failures can lead to a multitude of responses, ranging from noble to damaging to out-right bizarre. People sometimes commit to helping others purely out of guilt for their past failures. In past centuries, many engaged in self-harm to try to atone for their sins. Even modern Christians face the temptation, albeit much more subtly, to try to "make it up to God" by doing something we think he will appreciate: reading an extra chapter in the Bible, saying things that sound more spiritual, putting a little extra in the offering plate, or some other gesture we view as godly. Most are a waste of time and effort.

Certainly we should have some sort of proactive response to failure. Confession is necessary and proper. An effort to avoid repeating mistakes should be made. But, ultimately, our hope lies in the atonement and sacrifice of Christ. Understanding what he has already done for us frees us to respond in a healthy manner and move toward a life of overcoming the sin that persists, rather than getting caught in a vicious cycle of frustration, confusion, and defeat. Once we know that the only sufficient sacrifice has already been made, we have a better idea of where to go from there. But before we can fully understand the promise of sacrifice, we must first understand exactly why we need it in the first place.

Understanding the Need

There's a popular misconception regarding what we collectively call *sin*. It is the idea that all sins are equal. They are not. All are failure to one degree or another, but God can certainly distinguish between snapping at someone out of impatience and gunning him down in cold blood. So should we.

The Bible differentiates between the words we translate as *sin*, *transgression*, and *iniquity*. Psalm 32:5 says, "I acknowledged my sin to You, / And my iniquity I did not hide; / I said, 'I will confess my transgressions to the LORD'; / And You forgave the guilt of my sin." The tendency is to read all of these terms as synonyms, as interchangeable expressions of identical ideas, but in the Hebrew, they are three different words carrying three distinguishable meanings: *chata'ath* translated as "sin," *pesha'* translated as "transgression," and *'avon* translated as "iniquity." The Greek carries these same ideas in the words *hamartia*, *paraptoma*, and *adikia*.

The definition of *chata'ath* or *hamartia*, or "sin," describes when we wander from the path, miss the mark, or fail to do something we should. There is an element of "to err is human" here. When our mistake is one of *chata'ath*, we may be sinning unintentionally or out of ignorance. It is wrong and needs correction and covering, but it's not as problematic as it's often portrayed. God can deal with it. In fact, he's ready and willing when we ask.

To illustrate this, consider my friend and me hopping the wall at the Austrian castle. If someone had seen us wandering around the outside and said, "You're not supposed to be here," then we would have known we were in the wrong place. We would have asked the way to the entrance and gone in properly. This is sin: We go our own way, often out of ignorance, and end up in the wrong. We don't know we're wrong until it's pointed out to us.

Paul said that "through the Law comes the knowledge of sin" (Rom. 3:20). He also asserts that before the law was given, the sin that was in the world wasn't held against those people (Rom. 5:13). In our illustration, it's like saying that we were not liable for the admission fee until we saw the entrance gate and realized we were supposed to pay. By giving the Mosaic law to his people, God put up a big sign so mankind would know when they were walking the wrong way.

"Transgression," on the other hand, carries a greater weight. Paul wrote, "You were dead in your *trespasses* and *sins*" (Eph. 2:1, emphasis added), using both *paraptoma* and *hamartia*, respectively. Transgression—*pesha'* in the Hebrew or *paraptoma* in the Greek—carries a level of premeditation when crossing a line. It's more commission than omission. When we know that we should do something but don't, it is

24

sin. When we know that we should *not* do something but go ahead and do it anyway, it is transgression.

If my friend and I had seen a No Trespassing sign anywhere around the castle, we would not have gone the way that we did. There wasn't one; I promise. No arrows, no entrance signs, no *Kein Übertreten*. But if there had been and we had seen it, then glanced around to see if anyone was watching before we climbed the wall and entered the castle anyway, that would have been transgression. The sign, like the law, would have told us we were on the wrong path. If we had kept going, it would not have just been ignorant wandering; it would have been intentional trespassing.

As it was, our unintentional circumvention of the paid entrance, which was sin, led to us walking away and not paying even after we realized our mistake, which was transgression. Once we had gotten away with it, we never looked back. Uncorrected sin tends to lead to more intentional transgression. This lawlessness needs forgiveness, just as sin does, but it also needs redemption. Paul said that Jesus "gave Himself for us to redeem us from every lawless deed" (Titus 2:14). Christ is not only the sacrifice for our sins but the redeemer of our transgressions.

Finally, there's the serious condition of "iniquity" (*adikia* in the Greek; *'avon* in the Hebrew). The prophet Micah said, "Woe to those who scheme iniquity, / Who work out evil on their beds! / When morning comes, they do it, / For it is in the power of their hands" (Mic. 2:1). Paul wrote, "For the wrath of God is revealed from heaven against all ungodliness and unrighteousness of men who suppress the truth in unrighteousness" (Rom. 1:18). A pattern of purposeful unrighteousness or wrongdoing, plotted and carried out, indicates a deeper level of depravity. There is no repentance in the heart or mind of the one walking in iniquity.

Imagine if we had taken up residence in that castle after sneaking in the back way. The Austrian police would have shown up and ordered us to leave. But if we responded, "This isn't your castle; it's ours. We're not leaving, because we live here now!" that would have been iniquity. It denies the proper owner's authority, just as those who live in iniquity deny God's laws of right and wrong. Iniquity is defiant, arrogant, and stubborn. This requires more than a mere sacrifice. It demands forgiveness, redemption, and salvation.

In the case of all three types of failure that we tend to lump together as *sin*, there is both good news and bad news. First the bad news: All separate us from the righteousness of God. When it comes to perfection, it doesn't matter if you miss by an inch or a mile; you fall short every time. The good news is that God had a plan in mind from the beginning to counteract this bad news, and that plan came to its fullness in the promise of sacrifice.

Origin of the Sacrifice

The concept of sacrifice appeared early in the Bible. Cain and Abel each brought an "offering" to God, and Noah brought a "burnt offering." In Genesis 31 Jacob brought a "sacrifice" to initiate a peace covenant between him and his uncle Laban, and then in Exodus 24 God commanded Moses to offer a sacrifice to ratify God's covenant with Israel and the giving of the law. Covenants were only in force when blood was shed, and this particular type of sacrifice initiated a solemn agreement. It was a relational promise bound by the shedding of blood.

The ritualistic sacrifices we find later throughout the Old Testament were largely reminders of this covenant established on Mount Sinai. As more laws developed, the sacrifices and offerings became more complex and detailed. Let's look more closely at a few of them.

The peace offering showed gratitude to God for his provision and mercy. A portion was burned on the altar, a portion went to the priests, and the rest was eaten by the family of the one bringing the offering. Everyone participated in and benefited from this type of offering. It had no relation to sin. Interestingly, the series of rabbinic teachings known as the Talmud state that this is the only type of sacrifice that should continue to be offered once the Messiah has come.

The sin offering was made not to grant forgiveness for a sin but so the blood of the offering would cover sin in the life of the one bringing the sacrifice. These were for unintentional sins committed through carelessness, not willful acts of wrongdoing. The bigger the accidental sin, the bigger the size of the sacrifice. Some were made individually and some communally. In most cases, the priests ate the offering.

The guilt offering was made to cover a breach of trust or if someone thought he may have sinned but wasn't sure. If it was later discovered that a sin had actually taken place, then a sin offering would be brought. Again, the priests ate these.

Food and drink offerings signified the fruits of one's labor, giving the first portion of it back to God. Part of this offering was burned on the altar, and the rest was eaten by the priests.

There is a long list of other types of offerings, but these few were the most common.

In all cases, an offering did not obtain forgiveness for the one bringing it. The sacrificial system was never designed to atone for sin. The root of the Hebrew term *qorbon*, which is a broad term for "offering" or "sacrifice," means "to draw near."[1] God asked for sacrifices and offerings not to eliminate sin but to cover it, to institute giving, to illustrate the concept of a substitution, and to draw his people closer to him. In all cases, they were reminders of the covenant.

As important as the sacrifices were to the Israelites, they were imperfect, just like the old covenant. If the first one had been perfect, there would be no need for a new one. In fact, throughout the Old Testament, God revealed the insufficiency of sacrifices and offerings. Samuel said, "Has the LORD as much delight in burnt offerings and sacrifices / As in obeying the voice of the LORD? / Behold, to obey is better than sacrifice, / And to heed than the fat of rams" (1 Sam. 15:22). King David wrote, "For You do not delight in sacrifice, otherwise I would give it; / You are not pleased with burnt offering. / The sacrifices of God are a broken spirit; / A broken and a contrite heart, O God, You will not despise" (Ps. 51:16–17). Proverbs says, "To do righteousness and justice / Is desired by the LORD more than sacrifice" (21:3). This is echoed by the prophets Amos, Hosea, Micah, Isaiah, and others. Jeremiah even pointed out that offerings and sacrifices were not the purpose of the original Sinai covenant: "For I did not speak to your fathers, or command them in the day that I brought them out of the land of Egypt, concerning burnt offerings and sacrifices. But this is what I commanded them, saying, 'Obey My voice, and I will be your God, and you will be My people; and you will walk in all the way which I command you, that it may be well with you'" (Jer. 7:22–23).

No amount of personal sacrifice, even such as instructed under the ancient law, can make up for our imperfections. Gestures to make amends are just that: gestures. Here's the heart of God: He doesn't want our sacrifices. He doesn't want to condemn us. He doesn't want us to waste time and effort trying to atone for our sins. He wants fellowship in our hearts and obedience in our actions.

The sacrifices of the Old Testament were merely an illustration of the reality to come, which was the final sacrifice of Jesus Christ. The good news is that his sacrifice covers all of our failures. He offers forgiveness, redemption, and salvation; and when we accept the gift of his sacrifice, we are born into new natures through the obedience of faith, which wipes away our old selves and mistakes. Where we fail, Christ succeeds.

The book of Hebrews says, "Now once at the consummation of the ages He has been manifested to put away sin by the sacrifice of Himself" (9:26). The old eon was brought to a satisfying conclusion through the sacrifice on the cross, which validated the new covenant and brought us into a new era.

We live in this age. It is the age of Christ, the final sacrifice and full atonement for our sin. Any tendency to deny this fact pulls us back toward the shadow system under the law, but we are called to walk in the full light of the Messiah's revelation. If the sacrificial system had been sufficient to forgive sin, then there would have been no need for Christ to sacrifice himself on the cross. But since the blood of animals was not able to cover us, Christ had to destroy sin and make us perfect in the eyes of God. The priests could not make the Israelites clean, and the law couldn't reconcile them to God. But Jesus Christ made himself the perfect and final sacrifice and "now where there is forgiveness of these things, there is no longer any offering for sin" (Heb. 10:18).

This is the promise of the sacrifice: Christ is sufficient to forgive our sin, correct our transgression, and cleanse our iniquity.

Paid in Full

Sadly, the triumph of Christ's sacrifice and the truth that he died for the sin of the world have been twisted through the years into the false notion that this means there is now no more sin or that all sin is automatically forgiven. This teaching of universalism denies the need to consciously choose faith in Christ, learn his voice, and willfully obey. The consistent message of the New Testament, written after Christ's crucifixion, resurrection, and victory over sin, tells another story.

Paul taught that we all owe a debt we cannot pay, because "all have sinned and fall short of the glory of God" (Rom. 3:23). Peter said that when we don't know Christ, we are "continually straying like sheep" (1 Peter 2:25). Most of us have never tended a fold of sheep, but trust me when I tell you that they are *not* the smartest of animals. Without a shepherd, they drift aimlessly, lost and vulnerable. People are not much brighter. The idea of "being true to yourself" is terrible advice without the guidance of the Holy Spirit. Just look at the mess we make when we wander off on our own. It doesn't take a genius to know that foolishness, immorality, and downright evil come naturally to mankind and that we will not change without divine intervention. We desperately need a way out, and we can't earn it on our own. And that way out has been given to us through Jesus' sacrifice.

Once we have accepted his all-sufficient sacrifice, there should be a noticeable shift in the way we choose to live our lives. John wrote, "Whoever believes that Jesus is the Christ is born of God" (1 John 5:1). He also made the seemingly paradoxical claims that "if we say that we have no sin, we are deceiving ourselves and the truth is not in us" (1 John 1:8), and "We know that no one who is born of God sins" (1 John 5:18). The confusion that often happens here is due to a deficiency in the English language, not to conflicting truths. The Greek connotation in the verb of the latter verse denotes an ongoing lifestyle of sin. So what John was really saying was that we have already sinned in the past, but once we are reborn, we should not continue in that old lifestyle.

Before believing that Christ is the Messiah, we "practice sin." And you know what they say: practice makes perfect! We're naturally good at it, so good that it takes reams of laws and constant social pressure just to keep the majority of us from doing unbearable things. And that's barely enough to enable us to live together in a community. It still leaves us far from perfect, especially in the eyes of a perfect God.

Once we have faith in Christ, we still sin and sometimes transgress, but one who has been born of the Spirit is not capable of the remorseless and defiant type of sin the Bible calls *iniquity*. If someone is practicing iniquity, that person needs to check his spiritual birth certificate, because when John said, "No one who is born of God sins," that's what he was talking about. Once we've been made new by Jesus' sacrifice, we don't live lives in direct opposition to God, because that is no longer in our nature.

Because I understand these original concepts of what we collectively call *sin*, I am frequently baffled when people who claim to know and follow Christ seem to affirm those who are living in brazen iniquity. Today, it is popular to accept homosexuality or take a soft position on something such as abortion. Homosexuality is a huge red flag indicating that someone does not know God. Romans 1 makes it very clear that it is the direct result of rejecting God. Far from the person who struggles with same-sex attraction and may transgress at times, those who wholly embrace such a lifestyle proudly walk in iniquity.

From the outside, it can be hard to tell the difference. Repeated transgression can look like iniquity. But the one who is battling temptation is in a relatively good place compared to the one who has given himself or herself over to it. The believer knows the difference between right and wrong, while those apart from the Holy Spirit call wrong right. A Christian can struggle, but the one who lives a lifestyle in purposeful wrongdoing demonstrates that he does not know Christ. Paul called this lifestyle one of "degrading passions" that are "unnatural" and "depraved" (Rom. 1:26, 28). Why would a Christian ever affirm, excuse, or dismiss such a damaging practice?

Don't get me wrong—I go out of my way to show love and grace to my friends who are gay. But it's never at the expense of truth. We should never "give hearty approval to those who practice" such things, as Paul put it (Rom. 1:32). Those who affirm such a lifestyle do so to the great detriment of the person to whom they believe they are showing compassion. Jesus was the most compassionate person to ever walk the earth, but he did not shy away from speaking the truth, in love, to anyone. Neither should we.

The same principle applies when it comes to other social issues that have often been treated one-dimensionally by the church. Something that is clearly wrong, such as abortion, divorce (in most cases), or drug abuse, should be condemned by believers. But there is a huge difference between condemning the wrong and condemning the person. Some of those in the church have been guilty of coming down so hard on ungodly behavior that they have forsaken compassion for those engaged in the behavior. This is tragic and often counterproductive. The proper attitude is, of course, summed up perfectly in Jesus Christ.

When he encountered a woman living in iniquity who was facing death at the hands of the one-dimensional, law-abiding Jewish leaders, he sent her accusers packing by writing something in the dirt. What it was we don't know. Regardless, once he got her out from under the oppression of the practitioners of empty self-righteousness, he said something to the adulterous woman that sums up the right approach: "I do not condemn you, either. Go. From now on sin no more" (John 8:10–11).

This is one of the most beautiful and powerful exchanges in the entire Bible. It is a role model for how every believer should approach those living in iniquity. Jesus sought to redeem the woman, while urging her to forsake her ungodly practice. The phrase "Hate the sin, love the sinner" is often mocked by those who don't know God, but it precisely embodies the truth of Jesus Christ. Sin destroys, but Christ redeems. Sin is a cancer, and who would excuse, enable, or affirm cancer? At the same time, we love the person being destroyed by the cancer. The same is true with sin. We don't kill sinners or cancer patients; we do everything in our power to eradicate the deadly disease for the very purpose of saving the person.

The goal should always be that of redemption, which comes through the perfect sacrifice of Jesus Christ on the cross. We cannot sacrifice enough, nor can we make others sacrifice enough, to satisfy the righteous penalty of ungodly actions. The only hope for salvation comes through Jesus Christ, and he guarantees that his sacrifice is enough, regardless of our imperfections.

Once we come to Christ, our sins are "as far as the east is from the west" (Ps. 103:12). We consider ourselves "dead to sin, but alive to God in Christ Jesus" (Rom. 6:11). When we do this, we need not make continual sacrifices in feeble attempts at atonement. Our atonements have been made. Our decisions to live lifestyles of obedience, then, should be natural outworkings of our being made new. Paul told the believers in Philippi to "work out your salvation with fear and trembling; for it is God who is at work in you, both to will and to work for His good pleasure" (Phil. 2:12–13). Again, practice makes perfect. Instead of focusing on our shortcomings, we should accept that the final sacrifice has been made and get on with practicing obedience to the perfection of our faith.

Exposing the Lies

In Revelation 12:10, Satan is called the "accuser of our brethren," because he continually speaks the lie that sin is in charge and acts as a lord over us. The truth is the exact opposite. Our Lord rules over sin. The same passage fully says, "Now the salvation, and the power, and the kingdom of our God and the authority of His Christ have come, for the accuser of our brethren has been thrown down" (Rev. 12:10). Satan had his butt royally kicked. He still runs his mouth, but we need not listen to his lies. His only trick is deception, so when we know the truth by knowing the One who is Truth, he has no power.

This is not to minimize the impact of sin in our lives but to emphasize the power of God's forgiveness and sacrifice. We tend to obsess over, dwell on, and wallow in our sins, but they really need to be burned on the altar of the cross. Certainly we must acknowledge wrongdoing, but we must simultaneously acknowledge that when we lay sin before God, he exercises his authority to annul its power and blot it out of our lives. It is we who give it power when we listen to the lies, but it is he who crushes its potency.

This leads us to another misconception about Christ's sacrifice: that it was made to satisfy some blood lust on the part of God. This is simply not true. Jesus did not give up his life to comply with some demand of the devil. Jesus went to the cross willingly, even though he wrestled with it at Gethsemane. As he was teaching some hostile Jewish leaders, he told this parable:

> "I am the good shepherd; the good shepherd lays down His life for the sheep. He who is a hired hand, and not a shepherd, who is not the owner of the sheep, sees the wolf coming, and leaves the sheep and flees, and the wolf snatches them and scatters them. He flees because he is a hired hand and is not concerned about the sheep. I am the good shepherd, and I know My own and My own know Me, even as the Father knows Me and I know the Father; and I lay down My life for the sheep. I have other sheep, which are not of

this fold; I must bring them also, and they will hear My voice; and they will become one flock with one shepherd. For this reason the Father loves Me, because I lay down My life so that I may take it again. No one has taken it away from Me, but I lay it down on My own initiative. I have authority to lay it down, and I have authority to take it up again. This commandment I received from My Father." (John 10:11–18)

Jesus made it clear that his life was his own to give—and to take back up again. Satan didn't kill Jesus. God didn't kill Jesus. Not even the Romans who carried out the crucifixion or the Jews who turned him over to the Romans and demanded his execution killed Jesus. He took it upon himself to be a blood sacrifice and enact a new covenant between God and his people.

Give till It Hurts

What does the concept of sacrifice mean now that we're living under the freedom and promise of Jesus' ultimate and final sacrifice? Is that promise still relevant in our daily lives? One way we sometimes see people invoke the concept of sacrifice today is in cajoling people to give more money to a church or ministry than they might normally be inclined to give. They say, "Give till it hurts!" or they call it "sacrificial giving," which certainly sounds more spiritual. This use—or abuse—of *sacrifice* may have made sense during Old Testament times, but it's not applicable in the era of Christ. In Christ many things, including giving, are less about sacrifice and more about obedience and joy.

While Jesus was here on earth, he reminded the Jewish leaders of God's Word through Hosea: "'I desire compassion, and not sacrifice'"

(Matt. 9:13). He validated a scribe who quoted Jesus' own words back to him: "To love [God] with all the heart and with all the understanding and with all the strength, and to love one's neighbor as himself, is much more than all burnt offerings and sacrifices" (Mark 12:33). He did not condemn the Jews of his day who carried out the old covenant customs but pointed them toward something greater than tradition, toward questions of the heart.

In the book of Acts, after Christ's resurrection and ascension, Paul participated in a ritual of purification and sacrifice with some Jewish believers who were still under a vow to the law. He did so at the suggestion of the apostles in order to quell the accusation that he was teaching apostasy regarding the Mosaic law (21:26). He also circumcised Timothy to avoid confrontation with Jewish leaders as they sought to preach the gospel of Christ to all of the nations of Israel (Acts 16:3).

Realize that Paul was living in that time of transition, where the old structures of heaven and earth had not yet fully passed away. His choices did not mean he was advocating the sacrificial system for generations that would succeed him. His numerous writings on the subject clearly indicate that he understood the shift that was taking place around him as the old promises and prophecies played out. So as we think about what the promise of sacrifice means for us today, we need not feel bound to follow the rituals of old-covenant law or manufacture a new set of rituals ostensibly from the new covenant.

The only sacrifices instructed in the post-crucifixion age are metaphorical. The writer of Hebrews said, "Through [Christ] then, let us continually offer up a sacrifice of praise to God, that is, the fruit of lips that give thanks to His name. And do not neglect doing good and sharing, for with such sacrifices God is pleased" (13:15–16). Likewise, Paul said to the Romans, "Therefore I urge you, brethren, by the mercies of

God, to present your bodies a living and holy sacrifice, acceptable to God, which is your spiritual service of worship" (Rom. 12:1).

The clarion call of the Old Testament sacrifice to the New Testament believer can be summed up in these verses:

> Let us draw near with a sincere heart in full assurance of faith, having our hearts sprinkled clean from an evil conscience and our bodies washed with pure water. Let us hold fast the confession of our hope without wavering, for He who promised is faithful; and let us consider how to stimulate one another to love and good deeds. (Heb. 10:22–24)

Sacrifice in this age of promise has to do with our hearts and the good works that overflow from them. Good works do not produce salvation, but salvation produces good works. What then is a *good work*? Anything done in obedience to the Holy Spirit that is discernable in our souls and visible in our actions. It is not formulaic; it is individual. However, it is not arbitrary; it is consistent with Scripture.

So what about giving? First of all, it shouldn't be painful. Even the widow who gave out of her poverty did so with joy. If it hurts to give, you're probably doing it out of an Old Testament idea of sacrifice, which is clearly not what God wants. He'd rather you love and obey him and show compassion and love toward others. Of course, once you are operating out of love, compassion, and obedience, you may give much more than you do now. Instead of grudgingly giving 10 percent of your income to appease a portion of the old-covenant law (which was actually 20 percent in most years, and 30 percent in festival years),[2] you will happily give whatever the Holy Spirit leads you to give. That may even mean 100 percent, as in the case of the rich young ruler, but the so-called sacrifice will be constructive, not destructive.

There is ongoing debate in theological circles as to whether the Old Testament practice of tithing should still be operative today. Really, this should be irrelevant in the lives of believers because giving should be the norm: giving to support ministers in their work, giving to help those in need, and giving to build the kingdom of heaven here on earth. It should be an honor to give to the church, not an obligation. It should be delightful to help those in need, not dreadful.

Giving is not a sacrifice in the sense of Old Testament sacrifices. Instead, it is the natural response of those who understand the full atonement made by Christ on the cross and the role finances may play in building his kingdom on earth. We should never be manipulated by guilt, which is a sign that we're living under old-covenant mind-sets. The only motivation behind giving should be to express thankfulness for Jesus' sacrifice and to walk in obedience to the daily leading of the Holy Spirit.

Living the Promise

The promise of the sacrifice allows us to move beyond attempts to atone for our sins and live in the unearned grace that Christ made possible through his supreme and final sacrifice. Let's stop trying to pay for something that's already been bought and move on to the current task of building his priceless kingdom wherever we go.

Remember that you are alive in him! Share that life with your world. Discover the joy of giving. Experience the blessings of obedience. Store up treasures in heaven. Aim high, knowing even when you miss, you are forgiven. Admit your failures, let them go, and keep pressing on.

CHAPTER 3

The Promise of the Law

For sin shall not be master over you, for you
are not under law but under grace.
ROMANS 6:14

"The mountains are calling and I must go." That's what John Muir, American naturalist and founder of the Sierra Club, once said. That's also what's on the only sticker I've ever put on my car.

I may live in a flat, hot, crowded part of Texas, but I'd rather be in the mountains. If I could afford to get out of Texas for the entire months of July and August, I'd gladly trade this muggy oven for the cool, dry air of the mid-range of the Rockies. I actually own a season pass for Vail Resorts, so every winter I spend time at as many of their resorts as I can, which usually means one or two. Park City, Keystone, Beaver Creek . . . it doesn't matter. As long as I can get at least five days on the slopes, it pays for the pass.

I'm a good skier, but I'm also a smart skier. Most of the time, anyway. I've been known to fly by a Slow Area sign when nobody was around, but for the most part, I don't ignore the signs. If a trail is closed, I've learned to stay off it. I once ducked a rope and ended up walking down a steep, rocky slope, which was not much fun in ski boots. Suffice to say, I now always stay inside the ski boundaries. Every year, I read about people getting caught in avalanches—usually very good skiers—and I don't plan on ever being in one of those news stories.

I have found that abiding by the rules doesn't diminish my fun. In fact, it enhances it because I'm not worried about getting into trouble. I don't have to wear a beacon, carry a compass, or worry about getting my ski pass revoked. I ski by the rules and have a great time.

It's the same for God's law. At first glance, God's law appears to be no fun, to hold no promise. After all, it's humanly impossible to live up to it. The Israelites failed miserably, and if we attempt to uphold all 613 of the Old Testament laws, then we will fail miserably as well. Jesus said that all of the law is summed up in two commandments: "You shall love the Lord your God with all your heart, and with all your soul, and with all your mind," and "You shall love your neighbor as yourself" (Matt. 22:37, 39). But can we even live up to that? No. Not all the time for a lifetime. We will drift out of bounds at some point.

We need something else. Another way. If the law—any law—could justify us in the eyes of God, then living by it would put salvation in our own hands. But the law, both old and new, is not there to give us the key to our own salvation, rather to demonstrate our deficiencies. In the end, it directs us to the one and only Savior, Jesus Christ.

So what purpose is there in following any law if the final takeaway is that we couldn't possibly ever fully follow it? What promise could the law possibly hold? It all comes down to training us in obedience. Obedience unlocks God's blessings in our lives. Salvation comes only through grace, but blessings come through obedience.

Origin of the Law

When God delivered his people out of Egypt after four hundred years of slavery, he called Moses up to Mount Sinai. For forty days and forty nights, the holy mountain was shrouded in a cloud, a symbol of God's glory. In that place, sanctified by the Creator of mankind and the Deliverer of his people, the promise he had made to Abram began to unfold:

> "Go forth from your country,
> And from your relatives
> And from your father's house,
> To the land which I will show you;
> And I will make you a great nation,
> And I will bless you,
> And make your name great;
> And so you shall be a blessing;
> And I will bless those who bless you,
> And the one who curses you I will curse.
> And in you all the families of the earth will be blessed." (Gen. 12:1–3)

In those words, spoken long ago to a man of great faith and intimate relationship with God, several distinct promises were laid out. First, Abram would be blessed by God, personally set apart from everyone else. Second, he would be remembered for his faith. Third, he would be the patriarch of a great nation. Fourth, he would be protected by God, and the treatment he received from others would be returned to them by God himself. Fifth, everyone on the face of the earth would be blessed through him.

And so Moses, through the lineage of Abraham's promised son, Isaac, came to that place where the promise of a great nation would come to pass. No longer slaves, the people of Israel would be given heavenly and earthly authority directly from God. His instructions were specific. Moses received detailed blueprints for the construction of the ark of the covenant and the tabernacle. Priests were named and their clothing prescribed. God installed a ritual of sacrifices. He initiated the use of incense and anointing oils. The Sabbath observances were ordered and the Ten Commandments chiseled in stone, dictated by God to his chosen servant. On that sacred mountain, the foundation of law was codified.

The purpose of these rules and rituals was explicitly stated by God: "I will dwell among the sons of Israel and will be their God. They shall know that I am the LORD their God who brought them out of the land of Egypt, that I might dwell among them; I am the LORD their God" (Ex. 29:45–46).

These instructions were detailed and clear. Yet before Moses could even deliver them, God's people shattered them. While Moses was still on the mountain, the Israelites crafted a statue of a calf made of gold, foreshadowing a pattern of spiritual harlotry that would repeat itself for the rest of the age. When Moses came down and witnessed the idol worship, he threw down the tablets he had carved in obedience to God. Moses called out, "Whoever is for the LORD, come to me!" (Ex. 32:26). Exodus tells us that only the sons of Levi came to him. Moses then instructed them to take the sword to the people, and they killed three thousand people that day. The next morning, Moses went back to Mount Sinai to make atonement for their sins. As he did, God's judgment fell on the rest of the Israelites.

Soon God replaced the tablets containing the Ten Commandments, this time cutting the stone with his own finger. He renewed his covenant with Moses and the people, and they began constructing the tabernacle according to God's plans. Once it was complete, God began revealing his laws to Moses.

The laws contained primarily in the books of Leviticus and Numbers cover a wide range of ordinances, including the rites of worship, sacrifices, feasts, atonement, and priestly duties. He addressed issues of health, morality, poverty, economics, workload, and leadership. Two years, two months, and twenty days later, the people of Israel packed up and left Sinai to pursue their promised land of Canaan. Soon after, the complaints began.

As they approached the place they were to inhabit, Moses sent twelve men to spy in the land. Ten feared for their safety, citing those who already lived in that beautiful place. Only Joshua and Caleb, the other two spies, urged the people to press forward and possess the land. But the people rebelled. They feared for their lives and, despite God's miraculous deliverance and constant provision on the journey, refused to move in. Consequently, they wandered in the desert until everyone who had been born in Egypt, with the exception of Joshua and Caleb, died. The rebellious and complaining Israelites never took hold of God's promise.

After a generation of infighting and the decree of more laws, Moses died, and Joshua was anointed by God to lead the people into Canaan. After a series of battles, they eventually defeated the previous inhabitants, and the land was divided among the tribes. Then, when Joshua died, Judah took over and led the people to capture Jerusalem.

Though the Israelites did finally possess the promised land (or at least most of it), their pattern of rebellion and idolatry continued. Many generations struggled under the law, never able to live up to it. Some men of faith, including Gideon, Samuel, David, and Solomon, would find favor with God despite their failures. For hundreds of years, prophets would call the chosen people back to their God and warn them of the consequences of disobedience. Through it all, the threads of a promised Messiah were woven.

In Genesis, it was said that the Messiah would bruise the head of the serpent. To Abraham, it was promised he would bless all the nations of the earth. From King David, a promised "branch" would come to save Judah and Israel. Allusions to the coming King echo through the Psalms and the Prophets. But for hundreds of years, the people could only cling to the law. Their religion provided their only hope.

Then, in this wilderness of religious ritual and human failure, came a voice: "Repent, for the kingdom of heaven is at hand" (Matt. 3:2). This man, John the Baptist, promised both judgment and salvation. In fact, he said, it was already here. God had come to earth. The old covenant was coming to a climax and a new covenant was being established. Religion was about to die so that man could live.

Throughout it all, a pattern of truth emerged. From these truths, we can begin to understand the role of law and how it relates to us today. When we see how laws fit in God's plan, we can joyfully embrace the laws that apply to us today and begin walking in their promise.

Covenants of Grace

As with so many of the promises of God, to truly understand the promise of the law we must look at the covenants established between God and man. The first major covenant in the Bible takes place after the great flood. Noah was "a righteous man, blameless in his time" who "walked with God" (Gen. 6:9). In a world full of corruption, God honored Noah's love for him, sparing Noah's family in the ark. After the waters subsided, Noah built an altar and offered a blood sacrifice of animals. God made a covenant with Noah and his descendants: "I establish My covenant with you; and all flesh shall never again be cut off by the water of the flood, neither shall there again be a flood to destroy the earth" (Gen. 9:11).

Here we see a pattern that would be repeated: Noah believed in God, God saved him, a blood sacrifice was offered, and God made a covenant with man. This was repeated throughout the rest of the Old Testament.

When God promised Abraham descendants as countless as the stars and a land that he would show him later, Abraham "believed in the LORD; and He reckoned it to him as righteousness" (Gen. 15:6). Abraham brought a blood sacrifice of animals, and God made a covenant with him. Paul, reflecting on this in his letter to the church in Galatia centuries later, wrote, "For if the inheritance is based on law, it is no longer based on a promise; but God has granted it to Abraham by means of a promise" (Gal. 3:18). Paul emphasized the fact that the Old Testament law, which didn't exist at the time of Abraham, was separate from the gracious promise of God. Abraham's righteousness came from faith, not obedience to a set legal code.

Even Moses and the people of Israel he shepherded experienced God's favor before the law. God interrupted Moses' quiet existence in exile, reminding him of those who had faithfully served God in the past. He said by way of introduction, "I am the God of your father, the God of Abraham, the God of Isaac, and the God of Jacob" (Ex. 3:6). He told Moses that he was about to deliver his people out of Egyptian slavery and take them to the promised land, fulfilling his covenant with Abraham. God expressed his care and favor for his people, promising to bring them out of bondage, long before he gave the law.

But even after their miraculous deliverance, the Israelites were hardly obedient. Their disregard for the gracious favor God had shown them resulted in death for some of them, but it did not make them any less God's chosen people. Their disobedience may have ended their time on earth, but they remained in the covenant relationship God had established. They just missed out on the blessings they might have experienced in this life.

Just prior to delivering the first laws, God said to Moses, "*If* you will indeed obey My voice and keep My covenant, *then* you shall be My own possession among all the peoples, for all the earth is Mine; and you shall be to Me a kingdom of priests and a holy nation" (Ex. 19:5–6, emphasis added). This was not a promise of salvation or deliverance—God had already performed that—instead, it was a promise of blessing. So, despite hundreds of years to come of his people's disobedience to the law, he would continue to call his people back to him, promising that if they would obey, then he would bless. This if-then construct outlines the promise of the law. If those who have already been saved will simply obey, then they will experience the blessings he has in store.

The Law Under Christ

When looking at references to the law in the New Testament, differentiating between the various kinds of rules within the law—a societal custom, divine command, legal decree, fact of nature, and the Pentateuch—can be a little confusing. The same Greek word conveys all of these ideas. Most translations will signify the Old Testament laws by capitalizing the word, but it takes context, logic, and discernment to know which we are still obligated to keep, which we have been released from, and which we should defy or ignore now that we are living in the new covenant.

When Christ said he came to fulfill the law, he was speaking of the Mosaic law. When he said to make friends quickly with your opponent at law, he was speaking of the local legal system. When the Pharisees asked why the disciples were picking heads of grain for food to eat on the Sabbath, which was not lawful, Jesus treated it not as divine instruction, but Jewish tradition. When Pilate told the Jewish leaders to judge Jesus by their law, he referred to Jewish statutes, not Roman law, and certainly not God's divine law. When Peter and the apostles said they should obey God rather than men, they were breaking godless men's legal decrees in preaching the gospel, but obeying the instructions of God. And when James spoke of the law of liberty, he invoked the truth of nature as God ordained it (James 1:25). Clearly we are not to live lawlessly or by our own random set of individual rules. So how do we know what is law for us and what is not?

A lawyer once asked Christ, "What shall I do to inherit eternal life?" Jesus answered with two more questions: "What is written in the Law? *How does it read to you?*" (Luke 10:25–26, emphasis added). Personal opinions about the law have created the broad spectrum of modern interpretations that color Christianity.

The lawyer questioning Jesus answered succinctly and correctly. He didn't quote the 613 laws of the Old Testament. He didn't quote Jewish tradition. He certainly didn't quote Roman law. He answered with the divine law of God: "Love the Lord your God with all your heart, and with all your soul, and with all your strength, and with all your mind; and your neighbor as yourself" (Luke 10:27).

Note that the lawyer's question had to do with inheriting eternal life, as in salvation. His answer pointed to faith, yet did not ignore the practical actions of loving your neighbor. It was both faith and works. Jesus didn't correct him, but affirmed him. At the same time, Paul vigorously argued that the requirement for salvation is faith and faith alone. He called the law our "tutor," which leads us to Christ (Gal. 3:24). The translation there is a bit misleading to us, because we think of a tutor as an instructor. But when Paul used the term, it had a different meaning. *Thayer's Greek Lexicon* explains it this way:

> Among the Greeks and the Romans the name was applied to trust-worthy slaves who were charged with the duty of supervising the life and morals of boys belonging to the better class. The boys were not allowed so much as to step out of the house without them before arriving at the age of manhood.[1]

The tutor, at the time of Paul's writing, was not the instructor. He was a guardian. It was part of his duty to make sure the young boys showed up for the teacher's instruction. When the boy became a man, the tutor was no longer needed. Once mature, there was no need for a tutor.

Christ is our instructor. The law was the guardian that made sure immature mankind saw the need for instruction. But now we are to live as mature adults, spiritually speaking. Paul explicitly said this to the church in Corinth: "in your thinking be mature" (1 Cor. 14:20). This eliminates the need for the law in the Old Testament sense, but it does not eliminate the need for divine instruction, boundaries, and principles. Just as Christ didn't strike the lawyer's assertion to "love your neighbor as yourself," he also didn't nullify right and wrong. He simply allowed us to bypass the tutor and, as mature believers, learn how to obey him directly.

Again, it is the obedience of faith that brings salvation. Paul wrote to the Romans, "A man is justified by faith apart from works of the Law" (Rom. 3:28). Later in the letter, he asked and answered a related question: "Shall we sin because we are not under law but under grace? May it never be!" (Rom. 6:15). He clarified the new relationship that people of faith have with rules by saying, "Now we have been released from the Law, having died to that by which we were bound, so that we serve in newness of the Spirit and not in oldness of the letter" (Rom. 7:6). Serving "in newness of the Spirit" means that as servants of Christ, we do not live according to the old letter ("the Law") but rather under a new law of obedience to the Holy Spirit, he who comes after salvation so we may carry out the will of God in our lives and on this earth.

The new covenant of Christ, consecrated by his blood sacrifice, allows for salvation through faith instead of works, while simultaneously enabling obedience through our works for his glory and our benefit. This is where Christianity comes alive. James's assertion that "faith without works is dead" (James 2:26) does not refer to the keeping of laws, but to the power of obedience to perfect our faith. Living works are those inspired by obedience, not imposed by law.

This is truly living. When we quit living by a set of rules in a futile attempt to earn God's favor or salvation but begin walking in obedience, we step into a newness of Spirit and a life rich in the power to impact the world for God. The Enemy would seek to put the yoke of religious, rule-following bondage back on us to make us guilt-ridden, miserable, and ineffective; but there is freedom, joy, and power when we walk freely in the blessings of obedience.

Remnants of the Law

Do you know the three cardinal rules of religion? First, Jews don't recognize Jesus. Second, Protestants don't recognize the pope. Third, Baptists don't recognize one another in a liquor store. This joke, which always elicits hearty laughter from those raised in churches like the one of my childhood, reflects a sad truth. Religion overemphasizes rules. "Don't drink, don't dance, don't chew—and don't date those who do." That's what I heard growing up. Unfortunately, such religion is empty. There may be wisdom buried within the admonitions (it's a terrible idea for Christians to date non-Christians), but the truth gets lost in a simplistic black-and-white mentality of dos and don'ts. Dead religion based on legalism emphasizes rules, but Christ always emphasized relationship. In the Sermon on the Mount, he explicitly told the crowd that relationship was the single defining aspect of his true followers.

In fact, in Matthew 7, he made it clear that it is more imperative to truly know him than it is to perform all the outward actions that make other people think we do:

> "Not everyone who says to Me, 'Lord, Lord,' will enter the kingdom of heaven, but he who does the will of My Father who is in heaven will enter. Many will say to Me on that day, 'Lord, Lord, did we not prophesy in Your name, and in Your name cast out demons, and in Your name perform many miracles?' And then I will declare to them, '*I never knew you*; Depart from Me, you who practice lawlessness.'" (Matt. 7:21–23, emphasis added)

Although this passage is often used by fire-and-brimstone preachers to frighten Christians, it speaks more to those who are part of a religious organization without any real knowledge of Christ. It's popular to respect the views of Jews, Muslims, Hindus, Buddhists, and others by implying that their paths to God are as valid as Jesus', but Jesus said that actions in the name of God are not sufficient for salvation. We can't follow enough rules to please God and should not be lulled into believing that legalism (even within presumably Christian sects) is an adequate substitute for a relationship with Jesus Christ.

Nor is it adequate to simply know *about* God. Knowing about someone is not the same as knowing someone. I have read nearly all of the writings of C. S. Lewis. I have read biographical accounts about him. I have seen *Shadowlands*, the movie about his life. But Lewis died before I was born. I may feel as if I know him, but I don't—and he certainly doesn't know me.

The same is true with Jesus Christ. Many people read his words in the Bible, read others' opinions of him, profess to follow him, and even follow certain rules such as the Ten Commandments. But they don't know him. In the end, he will say, "I don't know you."

The good news is that we really can know him. "My sheep hear My voice, and I know them, and they follow Me," Christ said (John 10:27). Building a relationship with Jesus is much like building a relationship with any other person in your life: it takes time, communication, and continual interaction. This is the law we are to follow today, not some leftover permutation of the Old Testament or religious tradition.

Sin All You Want To

While we have been freed from religious rule-following, the truth is that our thoughts and actions do matter. They have eternal consequences, both for us and for those around us. But they are not the ultimate determining factors of our lives. In the end, the only thing that matters is a real relationship with God through his only Son, Jesus Christ. As they say in business, it's not what you know; it's who you know.

My pastor has a saying, "When you're a Christian, you can still sin all you want to. God just changes the 'want to.'" It's a great way to communicate the fact that religion is about boundaries and restrictions, while Christianity is about a change of the heart. What makes the distinction between rules and relationship baffling to some people is that both can have the same effect on one's behavior.

A person bound by religiosity may get up every Sunday, go to church, sing the songs wholeheartedly, put money in the offering plate, and say "amen" during all the right parts of the pastor's sermon. A Christian living in complete freedom of thought and action may do the exact same thing. The difference is in their motivations. One person behaves that way because he or she believes that such actions are required in order to please God, while the other would simply rather do nothing else. External pressure may modify behavior, but an internal transformation achieves genuine change.

G. K. Chesterton wrote, "Let your religion be less of a theory and more of a love affair."[2] It's the difference between a woman having sex with her husband out of a sense of duty versus making love to him out of pure unbridled passion. Religion is about duty; Christianity is about passion.

Many couples live in a state of stifled cheating. They are unsatisfied in their marriages and fantasize about another. Of course, they will never admit to it, but in the darkest of nights, they think about that "other," the one who is willing to fulfill all of their desires. In the daylight, they are bound to their vows and committed to their spouse. While faithfulness is noble and right, to many it feels like a prison. They want to be good husbands or wives, but wayward desire pulls away their hearts.

Spiritually, many Christians feel the same way. They want to be holy and righteous in the eyes of God, but the perceived passage to godliness is through rules and restrictions. Granted, this helps a lot of people avoid life-destroying mistakes, but it circumvents the real issue: freedom. The beauty of true Christianity is that your "want to" completely changes. Pleasing God is no longer a discipline; it's a joy.

A man or woman so in love and satisfied with his or her spouse does not desire another because it's "the rule." Each lives free from adultery because there is no "want to." A truly loving and fulfilling relationship leaves no room for cheating because there is no desire for it.

To put it in financial terms, the idea of Bill Gates committing armed robbery is ridiculous, not because he doesn't want more money, but because he has no reason or desire to get it illegitimately. He has all the cash he needs because of his success in the business world.

In relationships, it's the same. When we get all we need out of a relationship, illegitimate means have no need to satisfy. This is true between a husband and wife and between the Creator and the created. Bill Gates isn't tempted to rob a bank, so the laws against robbery won't ever be used to impede or punish him. Religion imposes rules to achieve an end; Christianity renders rules irrelevant through a satisfying relationship.

Too many churches work backward. They focus on rules to modify behavior, as if external actions can force internal attitudes. Christianity focuses on the heart to modify the desire. When you step out of religion (or obedience to a set of laws) and into a real relationship with Jesus Christ, you find that your heart changes and, in the process, finds fulfillment and joy in doing what God wants for you. You may behave similarly to someone living according to religion's rules, but your heart is completely different. There is a tendency among Christians to replace the Old Testament law with a form of New Testament law. And though there is a definite code of conduct for believers in the age of Christ, the pure expression of it is as the fruit of relationship, not the reinstitution of law.

A life legislated by dos and don'ts is frustrating and demoralizing. It inevitably leads to downfall, usually in the form of failure, disillusionment, or despair. Scandals rock the religious world with troubling regularity: A priest molests a child. An evangelist defrauds his supporters. A pastor consorts with prostitutes. And these are just the obvious, overt sins. How many religious people battle pride, jealousy, or addiction?

Anytime I hear a preacher rage against a particular sin, I cannot help but wonder if he struggles with that very issue. Churches that focus heavily on rules and regulations tend to have a higher rate of failure. Paul wrote that all who rely on observing the law are under a curse (Gal. 3:10). The old-covenant laws show us it is impossible to live up to a set of rules. We all fall short in this life. We may aim for the bull's-eye, but we all miss the mark. Imposing more rules or simply trying harder to maintain them is an exercise in futility. We need a fundamental change in our natures, which only comes through the transformation of our minds through relationships with God Almighty. We're all defective. We need to send ourselves back to our Maker for repair.

How often have you thought, *I'll never be good enough for God*? In fact, when you live your life by rules, you won't ever be good enough. Rules expose your deficiencies. Jesus Christ, on the other hand, enlightens you with his sufficiency. God said to Paul, "My grace is sufficient for you, for power is perfected in weakness" (2 Cor. 12:9). This is not an excuse to embrace weakness, but a call to walk in his strengthening power.

Rules put your focus in the wrong place—be it an institution and its regulations or yourself and your inadequacies. A relationship puts your focus on Jesus Christ. While those who live strictly by the rules feel bound and oppressed, those who live purely by the Spirit of God feel exhilarated and refreshed. It is the difference between life and death, the difference between Christianity and the law.

Strange Behavior

Living by society's laws is considered normal, even though it is clearly schizophrenic when examined through the long lens of time. In America, slavery was once legal and accepted; now it is abhorred. Sodomy was illegal when I was a child; now it is celebrated. Bible readings were routine in public schools a century ago; now they can get you expelled. Society's laws change, sometimes in the right direction, sometimes in the wrong direction. Obedience to the Holy Spirit, however, is always right, even when it requires opposition to society's laws.

Laws can be strange. In Delaware, you can't sell the hair of a dog or cat unless it is cut in a commercial grooming establishment (seriously).[3] In New Hampshire, you can't collect "seaweed or rockweed from the seashore below high-water mark, between daylight in the evening and daylight in the morning."[4] I'm sure they have good reasons for those (I'm being generous here), but it illustrates how some laws just seem weird. The same is true when Christians behave as Christ instructed. To the world, it often seems weird.

God's rules are not natural. In Romans 12, Paul told Christians such unnatural things as "Bless those who persecute you" (v. 14), "Never pay back evil for evil to anyone" (v. 17), and "If your enemy is hungry, feed him, and if he is thirsty, give him a drink" (v. 20). These run counter to human nature. If you want to test this, just walk up to someone on the street and do something nasty, like spit in their face or insult them with crude remarks. See how many kind responses you get. The behavior Paul proposed flies in the face of our natural inclinations.

If you spit in a religious man's face, you may not get a violent response because his religion may have instilled a sense of self-restraint. But if his thoughts were broadcast across an unfiltered radio frequency, that station would likely be banned in most family-friendly places. External restraint is good, but it's not the goal of Christianity. The transformed heart doesn't repay "evil for evil" because it loves its persecutor.

This unnatural, internal condition cannot be achieved through guilt, manipulation, or any other contrived means. It can only come supernaturally, through a daily exercise in what theologians call "dying to self." This death is not an end; it is a beginning. "Whoever loses his life for My sake," Jesus said, "will find it" (Matt. 16:25).

Christianity is a resurrected life, where our human natures (with all of their destructive, self-centered, despicable tendencies) die, and new, more fulfilling lives through Christ arise. This cannot be imposed by any law or religious institution. Attempts to do so have led to the disillusionment of many people. The remedy lies in Jesus Christ, and the road to recovery begins at the foot of the cross, where our old natures die and we become new creatures.

The Law of Freedom

Christ followers are not under the law in the way that the Israelites were because we live in the age of a new covenant. The heavenly and earthly authority of the Mosaic covenant is obsolete because it was fulfilled in Christ. His blood sacrifice enacted a new covenant. Salvation comes by grace through faith. It is a gift freely given by God, not one earned by works.

The balancing truth to that great grace is that life in Christ is not lawless. It is true that we cannot undo what God has done by our works. Since we didn't earn salvation, we cannot unearn it. But clearly works play an important role. Jesus plainly said, "If you love Me, you will keep My commandments" (John 14:15).

Note the context of Jesus' statement. Just prior, he was instructing his disciples and talking about works: "He who believes in Me, the works that I do, he will do also; and greater works than these he will do; because I go to the Father" (John 14:12). *Works* is not used here in a striving-to-please-God sense. It's a promise of power and greatness through imitation and obedience. Those who believe in Christ will do as he did and even greater. It's hard to imagine doing anything greater than Christ, but he opens the door to just that and invites us to walk through it.

Jesus continued, "Whatever you ask in My name, that will I do, so that the Father may be glorified in the Son. If you ask Me anything in My name, I will do it" (John 14:13–14). This huge statement has troubled me at times. If it extends beyond the original disciples, why have so many people genuinely sought God's will in a situation, asked for something that would seem to glorify God, and not received it?

The eight Greek words (*hos aiteo onoma poieo hina pater doxazo huios*) that make up verse 13 could be rendered, "Whatever is needed for those under my authority, I will provide in order that the Father can magnify the Son." The key is the conjunction "in order that." Those who ask are not the focal point of the statement. It's not "whatever we ask for, we get," but "whatever we ask while under Christ's authority, he will provide in such a way that he is glorified."

The purpose of fulfillment is not to please the asker, but to allow Christ to be magnified. The key is in the relationship. Being "in Jesus' name" means operating under his command and authority. He wraps up that idea with the declaration, "If you love Me, you will keep My commandments." If you want to know the rule of Christianity, there it is. It comes down to the combination of relationship and authority. Live close to him, operate under his authority, and do what he asks.

Even though Jesus has made obedience under the new covenant simple, the urge to codify his commandments continues to this day. Why? Because obedience is intensely personal. Jesus told the rich young ruler to sell everything he had and give it to the poor. To one unnamed disciple whose father had just died, Jesus said, "Follow Me, and allow the dead to bury their own dead" (Matt. 8:22). Can you imagine making those absolute commandments? "XI. Thou shalt sell everything. XII. Thou shalt not bury thy dead." Given the way people take a few words and make them church doctrine, I'm surprised there's not a sect of Christianity somewhere that outlaws funerals. (For the record, it is generally accepted that the man's father was aging and the potential disciple wanted to be exempt from following Christ until his father died. Whatever the case, the quote "Allow the dead to bury their own dead" would make a pretty cool bumper sticker, if you ask me.)

Clearly, there are things Christians should do and things we should not do, but it is not because religious rules are literally chiseled in stone. Instead, a godly code of conduct is chiseled into our hearts and minds as we submit to the authority of Christ. Making these things laws to be externally enforced shifts the relationship from one of obedience to one of legalism.

That's why I often cringe at the motto What Would Jesus Do? Should we imitate Christ by gathering twelve disciples, preaching in synagogues, and dying an unmarried, childless man on a cross? Clearly not. The question is, "What would Jesus have *me* do?" We imitate Christ by seeking, hearing, and obeying the Father. Christianity then becomes more proactive than preventative. We aim for obedience and fire away. We sometimes miss the mark (a.k.a. sin), but when we do, we simply adjust and fire again.

Living the Promise

Because we are a little too much like sheep, Jesus did lay out some clear instructions. Granted, he said most of them to specific people at a specific time for a specific purpose, but we can still glean the Father's heart from most, if not all, of them. Take the rich young ruler. The lesson should be that we are to value Jesus Christ more than money. That may require selling and giving everything, but it may not. Or take what Jesus told Peter about forgiving the person who offended him 490 times (seven times seventy). This doesn't mean we should tabulate our forgivenesses until we cross that threshold. It means we should live lives of forgiveness. Jesus also said we should go two miles when required to go only one. That means going beyond our obligations to help people, which creates an opportunity for sharing his love. He said to seek first his kingdom, which means prioritizing heavenly things and bringing his kingdom to earth. He said multiple times to love one another, which is a natural expression rather than a legalistic task when we truly love him.

When faith is alive, it always produces good works. Not works of our own that may be considered good, but works of obedience inspired by the Holy Spirit. Herein lies the fulfillment of the promise of the law. When obedience is written on our hearts and put into action, it perfects our faith, changes those around us, and opens the blessings of heaven.

CHAPTER 4

The Promise of the Chosen People

But you are a chosen race, a royal priesthood, a
holy nation, a people for God's own possession.
1 PETER 2:9

I was adopted. After giving birth to my older sister, my mother was told she would not have any more children. My parents wanted a son, so when their lawyer friend mentioned that he knew a doctor with an expectant mother who could not care for her son, they began legal proceedings to adopt me at birth.

Adoption is not inherently good or bad. But it does make you different. Throughout my childhood, I joked with my sisters (my mother had another child later, surprising everyone) that I was chosen, but our parents were stuck with them. Let's face it: My parents were under zero obligation to adopt me. They didn't know me. The expenses they incurred, the time they invested, and the liabilities they assumed were (and still are) pure grace. I did nothing to earn it or deserve it. I was, quite obviously, chosen.

Most religious groups also feel chosen. They consider themselves special, unique, or even exclusive. Who we believe is chosen by God impacts how we view others and ourselves. It also drives how we treat others. There are many Christians today who believe that modern-day Jews, whether by birth or by conversion, are set apart by God. There are even those who see two paths to salvation—one for Jews and another for Gentiles, or non-Jews. If they are still God's chosen people, as they are clearly called in the Old Testament, then they should be treated as such. If not, then perhaps the greatest disservice we could do is to treat them differently. Of course, no scenario justifies the persecution they have endured as a people, but the question of their eternal status is significant.

Being set apart by God for a purpose carries a special responsibility and unique promises. Religious and ethnic groups have argued about this for centuries. Who has God chosen as his people? How are people set apart in the world today? What does it even mean to be set apart? To understand the issue and apply it to our modern (and future) worldview, we must journey back to the time of Abram and the birth of the nation called "chosen" by God in ancient times.

The Original Chosen

God appeared to Abram, as he was then called, when he was the ripe age of ninety-nine, and told him that he would make Abram the "father of many nations." This promise held a haunting irony. Though *Abram* meant "great father," he and his wife had been unable to have children. Wanting a son, Abram had taken his wife's Egyptian slave,

Hagar, and conceived Ishmael, which means "God hears." Because of his illegitimacy, God said he would be "a wild donkey of a man" and that everyone would fight with him. He would be cursed to live in hostility toward his brothers (Gen. 16).

Thirteen years later, God's promise of a great lineage came with the command to walk faithfully with God and "be blameless" (Gen. 17:1). God changed Abram's name to Abraham, meaning "father of many," and made a promise to him and his family line: "I will establish My covenant between Me and you and your descendants after you throughout their generations for an everlasting covenant, to be God to you and to your descendants after you" (Gen. 17:7).

So the one-hundred-year-old man and his ninety-year-old wife had a son. As God instructed, they named him Isaac, which means "he laughs," for Abraham and Sarah both laughed when God suggested the aged couple would bear their first and only child.

Once grown, Isaac married Rebekah, and they had twin sons, Esau and Jacob. When Isaac was old and blind, Jacob deceived his father to gain the family blessing. "May peoples serve you," Isaac said, believing he was speaking over Esau, "And nations bow down to you; / Be master of your brothers, / And may your mother's sons bow down to you. / Cursed be those who curse you, / And blessed be those who bless you" (Gen. 27:29).

When his deception was discovered, Jacob fled to the land of his mother to find a wife for himself. After working for seven years to obtain the hand of Rachel, he was deceived on his wedding night and consummated his marriage with her older sister, Leah. His own deception had come full circle.

The next day, he discovered his mistake and protested to Laban, the father of both girls. Laban agreed to give him Rachel as well, so Jacob took both as wives. Leah gave him six sons: Reuben, Simeon,

Levi, Judah, Issachar, and Zebulun. Rachel bore one son, Joseph. Jacob also fathered four other sons with his wives' servants. These were named Dan, Naphtali, Gad, and Asher. After twenty years, Jacob returned to Canaan with his two wives, eleven sons, and their servants. When he arrived, he wrestled with an angel one night, who told Jacob he would be called Israel from then on.

He later moved his family to Bethel, where Rachel bore his twelfth son, Benjamin, then died after giving birth. These twelve sons became the patriarchs of the twelve tribes of Israel.

Rachel's oldest son Joseph was sold into slavery by his brothers and taken to Egypt, where he eventually served Pharaoh and prospered. When famine struck Canaan, his brothers came to Egypt and settled in the region of Goshen as honored resident aliens. Jacob (Israel) came and lived with them as well. Before he died, he blessed Joseph's sons, Manasseh and Ephraim. But as had been the case with Jacob and Esau, the blessing was passed to the younger brother, Ephraim. Jacob promised that "his descendants shall become a multitude of nations" (Gen. 48:19).

Shortly after, the father of the Israelites gathered his twelve sons. After predicting the futures of each one, he died. The Israelites stayed in Egypt, and by the time at least four generations had passed, the tribes had grown rich and "increased greatly, and multiplied, and became exceedingly mighty, so that the land was filled with them" (Ex. 1:7). During that time, the pharaoh of Joseph's time died, and a new ruler came to power who did not like the Israelites and made them slaves. As they continued to multiply, his oppression became harsher. He worked them ruthlessly, but they remained fruitful. Eventually, he ordered all newborn male Israelites be put to death by being thrown into the Nile River. But one Levite boy survived. His name was Moses. In him the covenants of the past culminated in the promise of the Israelites becoming God's chosen people.

Set Apart

After Moses led the Israelites out of Egyptian bondage, he settled for a while at Mount Sinai, as we discussed previously, where God gave him the law and renewed his covenant with those he now called chosen: "For you are a holy people to the LORD your God; the LORD your God has chosen you to be a people for His own possession out of all the peoples who are on the face of the earth" (Deut. 7:6).

Why did God choose the Israelites to be his own people, to be set apart for him? The decision was certainly not based on their own merits. If anything, he chose them despite their actions. This demonstrated his faithfulness, not theirs, as he fulfilled his promise to Abraham and their other ancestors. They didn't deserve God's favor, but he chose them. He set them apart from all other nations as his own.

As he renewed his promise, he vowed to love them, protect them from their enemies, increase their numbers, bless their crops and herds, stave off disease, and give them a land to possess. But the blessings of being chosen came with a condition: the people were required to love God and keep his commandments. "Then it shall come about, because you listen to these judgments and keep and do them, that the LORD your God will keep with you His covenant and His lovingkindness which He swore to your forefathers" (Deut. 7:12).

This conditional relationship continued throughout the Old Testament. Breaking the covenant forfeited the blessings. When the Israelites failed, God was no longer bound by his promise. His words explicitly stated the premise that he would act only in accordance with their obedience. Being chosen was not merely a blessing, but a massive responsibility. "Know therefore that the LORD your God, He is God, the faithful God, who keeps His covenant and His lovingkindness to a thousandth generation with those who love Him and keep His commandments; but repays those who hate Him to their faces, to destroy them; He will not delay with him who hates Him, He will repay him to his face" (Deut. 7:9–10).

Obedience and faithfulness to the covenant were essential for the Israelites to experience the blessings of being chosen. Unfortunately, they were a fickle group. As I described in chapter 2, most of the generation delivered from Egyptian slavery never entered the promised land, because the people rebelled against Moses when ten of the twelve spies they sent to scout out the land returned in fear of the current inhabitants and advised against entering. In response, God said, "Surely you shall not come into the land in which I swore to settle you, except Caleb the son of Jephunneh and Joshua the son of Nun. Your children, however, whom you said would become a prey—I will bring them in, and they will know the land which you have rejected. But as for you, your corpses will fall in this wilderness" (Num. 14:30–32).

The fearful ten spies died of a plague. The rest wandered for forty years. Moses died in the valley of Moab and was buried by God himself. After forty years Joshua and Caleb, the only two spies who had responded in faith, led the Israelites into the promised land. The twelve tribes settled in Canaan and continued to win victories over the native pagan cities, enjoying the fruit of their obedience to the Lord.

But a generation after Joshua died, the Israelites "did evil in the sight of the LORD" and served other gods (Judg. 2:11). Just as he had promised, God turned against them. They no longer won battles over their enemies but instead suffered great defeats. God raised up judges to save his people from their enemies, but the people continuously "played the harlot after other gods and bowed themselves down to them" (Judg. 2:17). God withdrew from his chosen people and allowed the evil tribes to live among them. The Israelites intermarried with the Canaanites, Hittites, Amorites, Perizzites, Hivites, and Jebusites. They served pagan gods and eventually were sold into slavery.

Again, God called out a Moses-type leader to deliver the Israelites. The faithful spy Caleb had a nephew named Othniel whom God raised up as a warrior judge, and the people were once again delivered. But after forty years of peace, Othniel died and the Israelites fell into their old, evil ways. The Moabites conquered Israel and subjected them to slavery for the next eighteen years. God then raised up a Benjamite leader named Ehud, who deceived the Moabite king, cut him open with a sword, and led the battle against the Moabites. Peace reigned for eighty years that time, before the cycle began again.

For hundreds of years, virtually every generation failed to uphold God's covenant. A few individuals remained faithful, but the majority did not. Consequently, God's chosen people were enslaved until they cried out to God in despair. God relented and sent leaders such as Gideon, Jephthah, and Samson to deliver them. But afterward, the tribes continued arguing among themselves and marrying outside of their people.

Then, as God was raising up another prophet to speak to the people, the Philistines defeated the Israelites in battle and captured the ark of the covenant. After seven months of misery, the Philistines sent the ark back, and the prophet Samuel turned Israel back to God. He ruled in peace for the rest of his life and in old age appointed his two sons to lead. However, they were dishonest, and all the elders of Israel aligned against them. They demanded of Samuel a king, just as the other nonchosen people had. This grieved Samuel, but as he prayed to God over the matter, God said,

"Listen to the voice of the people in regard to all that they say to you, for they have not rejected you, but they have rejected Me from being king over them. Like all the deeds which they have done since the day that I brought them up from Egypt even to this day—in that they have forsaken Me and served other gods—so they are doing to you also." (1 Sam. 8:7–8)

Samuel warned the people that they would become slaves to a king, even if he was an Israelite. "Then you will cry out in that day because of your king whom you have chosen for yourselves, but the LORD will not answer you in that day" (1 Sam. 8:18).

But again they ignored the word of their God, so Samuel gave the nation of Israel their first king: Saul. And the story of the chosen people continued in its cyclical pattern. The covenant God had promised to Abraham and kept through Moses and various judges was overwhelmingly one way. God was faithful; the Israelites were not.

An Earthly Kingdom

The descendants of Jacob, after generations of spiritual prostitution, physical slavery, and foreign marriages, finally established their physical kingdom, calling it Israel. The Spirit of God fell on Samuel's chosen king, and Saul led them into battle against their current oppressors, the Ammonites. Once again, God delivered the tribes of Israel, but it came with a warning from his prophet. Samuel pointed out their rebellion in demanding a king. At the same time, he promised that if the people and their king would serve and obey God, they would be blessed. "Only fear the LORD and serve Him in truth with all your heart; for consider what great things He has done for you. But if you still do wickedly, both you and your king will be swept away" (1 Sam. 12:24–25).

Saul reigned for forty-two years, but he failed. God spoke to

Samuel, saying that he regretted making Saul king. God rejected Saul for his disobedience and instructed Samuel to choose a new king. Samuel went to Bethlehem, found David, and anointed him as the next king. After a time of treachery when Saul sought to kill David, he was wounded in battle and took his own life in despair. David rose to power, but only after a long period of infighting among the Israelites. After much blood was shed, David's faction achieved victory, and the new king united the tribes once again. King David reigned over all of Israel and Judah for thirty-three years.

In many of his psalms, David reflected on the blessings and burdens of being "chosen." Psalm 78 recounts the people's history from Moses to David, illustrating the Israelites' failure to uphold God's covenant.

> When He killed them, then they sought Him,
> And returned and searched diligently for God;
> And they remembered that God was their rock,
> And the Most High God their Redeemer.
> But they deceived Him with their mouth
> And lied to Him with their tongue.
> For their heart was not steadfast toward Him,
> Nor were they faithful in His covenant.
> But He, being compassionate, forgave their iniquity and did not
>   destroy them;
> And often He restrained His anger
> And did not arouse all His wrath.
> Thus He remembered that they were but flesh,
> A wind that passes and does not return. (vv. 34–39)

If not for the compassion of the Lord, the old covenant would have ended with the utter destruction of the Israelites. It wasn't their repentance or righteousness or even most-favored-nation status that prevented their extinction. It was nothing but the grace of God. David also wrote in that passage:

> He also drove out the nations before them
> And apportioned them for an inheritance by measurement,
> And made the tribes of Israel dwell in their tents.
> Yet they tempted and rebelled against the Most High God
> And did not keep His testimonies,
> But turned back and acted treacherously like their fathers;
> They turned aside like a treacherous bow.
> For they provoked Him with their high places
> And aroused His jealousy with their graven images.
> When God heard, He was filled with wrath
> And greatly abhorred Israel. (vv. 55–59)

That's a pretty damning account. The New International Version says God "rejected Israel completely" (v. 59). Keep in mind this was written by a man of faith. He understood that unbelief resulted in God's rejection and judgment, but that repentance restored the relationship because God remained faithful even when man did not.

Then, through the prophet Nathan, God made a promise to David:

> "When your days are complete and you lie down with your fathers, I will raise up your descendant after you, who will come forth from you, and I will establish his kingdom. He shall build a house for My name, and I will establish the throne of his kingdom forever. I will be a father to him and he will be a son to Me; when he commits iniquity, I will correct him with the rod of men and the strokes of

the sons of men, but My lovingkindness shall not depart from him, as I took it away from Saul, whom I removed from before you. Your house and your kingdom shall endure before Me forever; your throne shall be established forever." (2 Sam. 7:12–16)

This prophecy speaks of Solomon, who did a lot wrong—marrying foreign women and worshipping their gods—but is still known as the wisest ruler Israel ever had. And it may mention the Christ eventually to come, a descendant of David who would establish the eternal throne.

God would complete his portion of the covenant and give the Israelites a messiah. Because of the people's continued disobedience, they would see more judgment and hardship, from outside invaders to the split of the kingdom into two, to exile, captivity, and so much more. But, through it all, God's promise of restoration still came through:

"Behold, days are coming," declares the LORD, "when I will make a new covenant with the house of Israel and with the house of Judah, not like the covenant which I made with their fathers in the day I took them by the hand to bring them out of the land of Egypt, My covenant which they broke, although I was a husband to them," declares the LORD. "But this is the covenant which I will make with the house of Israel after those days," declares the LORD, "I will put My law within them and on their heart I will write it; and I will be their God, and they shall be My people. They will not teach again, each man his neighbor and each man his brother, saying, 'Know the LORD,' for they will all know Me, from the least of them to the greatest of them," declares the LORD, "for I will forgive their iniquity, and their sin I will remember no more." (Jer. 31:31–34)

From the shadows of the old age, the prophets saw the promise of the new. It was a glimpse of Christ to give hope for the future. Generations later, into this world of turmoil, violent clashes, and fighting against assimilation with the cultures of Israel's captors, the final King of the Jews was born.

Jesus and the Jews

Jesus came onto the scene at a time when the Jews held significant authority in Israel under the cover of Rome. The temple had been rebuilt, expanded, and was fully functional. Even so, their claim of being chosen people was scandalous. The Pharisees and Sadducees vied for power. The Samaritans still worshipped at Mount Gerizim, though there was no temple, and were reviled by the Jews. Despite generations of intermarrying, multiple diaspora, and an influx of nongenetic converts to Judaism, the claim of Jewishness was a point of pride, indicating racial and spiritual superiority.

In the early part of his ministry, Jesus embarked on a campaign of teaching in the Jewish synagogues. As he taught and performed miracles, traveling from place to place, he developed a reputation, and people came from all around to see him, including from areas outside of Judea (Matt. 4:23–25).

Jesus purposely targeted the Israelites first, because he was the fulfillment of the prophecies of a messiah. Yet he also extended salvation to those outside of the old covenant. He hinted at this when speaking to a group of Pharisees: "I have other sheep, which are not of this fold [meaning the Jews]; I must bring them also, and they will hear My voice; and they will become one flock with one shepherd" (John 10:16).

In another passage, Mark tells the story of a Syrian woman who found Jesus and pleaded with him to deliver her daughter from an evil spirit (Mark 7:25–30). At first he didn't even answer her because he wasn't making his presence known. He had previously told his chosen twelve to go exclusively to the Jews. "Do not go in the way of the Gentiles, and do not enter any city of the Samaritans; but rather go to the lost sheep of the house of Israel" (Matt. 10:5–6). Clearly his first priority was to the Jews. (It's interesting to note that he did not group the Samaritans with the Gentiles or the "house of Israel." The debate about their religious status was sensitive given their mixed ancestry and adherence to the Old Testament faith.)

Now he was being hounded by this Gentile woman, and the disciples wanted her sent away. Jesus responded, "I was sent only to the lost sheep of the house of Israel." But the woman would not relent. Finally, he said, "Let the children be satisfied first, for it is not proper to take the children's bread and throw it to the dogs." This curious response wasn't simply a callous insult. Jesus was reflecting the view of the Jews at the time. Women such as her were viewed as unclean under the law and not worthy of the divine. Jesus was on a mission to the "lost sheep" of Israel, who were the chosen children of God when this Gentile intercepted him. He acknowledged this dilemma in front of his disciples.

But the woman answered, "Yes, Lord, but even the dogs under the table feed on the children's crumbs." She would not be persuaded. This woman, though not chosen by birth, fully believed that Christ could deliver her daughter. And she was right.

Jesus responded, "Woman, your faith is great; it shall be done for you as you wish" (Matt. 15:21–28; Mark 7:24–30). The King of the Jews demonstrated that he would also be the King of the whole world.

Though this had to be surprising to the disciples, and deeply troubling to any Jewish leaders who heard about it, this wasn't the first time Jesus had gone beyond the "lost sheep of the house of Israel."

Previously, when Jesus was in Capernaum, a Roman centurion came to him and said, "Lord, my servant is lying paralyzed at home, fearfully tormented."

Jesus replied, "I will come and heal him."

But the centurion said, "Lord, I am not worthy for You to come under my roof, but just say the word, and my servant will be healed."

Jesus was so impressed with this Gentile's faith that he announced to the crowd that had gathered, "Truly I say to you, I have not found such great faith with anyone in Israel" (Matt. 8:10).

What a jarring statement! Could it really be possible that one who was not of the chosen tribes could have more faith than them? Not only did Jesus declare it, but he cast a sharp rebuke on those Jews who would reject him. "I say to you that many will come from east and west, and recline at the table with Abraham, Isaac and Jacob in the kingdom of heaven; but the sons of the kingdom will be cast out into the outer darkness; in that place there will be weeping and gnashing of teeth" (Matt. 8:11–12).

Here was a principle that would echo in the Gospels and the Epistles. Those who reject Christ, even if sons of the kingdom by birth, would be cut off and cast out. As in the Old Testament, those without faith in God, now manifest in Christ, would not inherit the blessings of the new covenant. Those who did have faith would be blessed.

"Go; it shall be done for you as you have believed." The centurion's servant was healed that very moment (Matt. 8:5–13).

No Longer Different

This powder-keg combination of elements in Jesus' ministry—claiming to be the divine Messiah, convincing people through miraculous works, and accepting Gentiles as well as Jews—led to the inevitable showdown with the religious leaders. Jesus didn't make it easy on them.

While teaching in the great restored temple in Jerusalem, Jesus said to the Jews who listened, "If you continue in My word, then you are truly disciples of Mine; and you will know the truth, and the truth will make you free" (John 8:31–32). In this statement was the implication that these chosen people weren't already free, to which they responded with this historically ignorant statement: "We are Abraham's descendants and have never yet been enslaved to anyone; how is it that You say, 'You will become free'?"

Jesus could have recounted the hundreds of years of Israelite slavery from Egypt to Assyria and Babylon to Rome, but instead he spoke in strictly spiritual terms: "Everyone who commits sin is the slave of sin." Then he crushed the idea that Jewishness equated to oneness with God: "The slave does not remain in the house forever; the son does remain forever."

How could it be that those who were chosen would not remain "in the house forever"? After all, God's old covenant had been an eternal one, passing down to all generations. Yet here was this teacher telling them that they needed something new from him. "So if the Son makes you free, you will be free indeed," he said.

Jesus acknowledged their genetic claim by saying, "I know that you are Abraham's descendants." He wasn't claiming they were not Jews. He was, however, claiming that lineage alone was not enough. "You seek to kill Me," he said, "because My word has no place in you."

As startling as this would have been, Jesus' assertion was not at odds with the promises God made to their forefathers. Every covenant, from the original one made at Mount Sinai to the renewed ones throughout the times of the judges, kings, and prophets, came with the condition that God would bless his people if they would obey his

Word. If not, he would cut them off. Of course, few ended up keeping God's commands. As a group, the chosen people had never given God's Word a consistent place of honor. That's why the Israelites suffered defeat at the hands of numerous invading armies and became foreign nations' slaves. Though they were enjoying some national autonomy under Rome as Jesus spoke to them, they were still enslaved to sin just as their forefathers were. But Jesus didn't stop at calling them slaves.

"I speak the things which I have seen with My Father; therefore you also do the things which you heard from your father," he said.

Again, they fell back to their earthly roots. "Abraham is our father," they said.

Jesus countered, "If you are Abraham's children, do the deeds of Abraham. But as it is, you are seeking to kill Me, a man who has told you the truth, which I heard from God; this Abraham did not do. You are doing the deeds of your father."

This had to sting. First, Jesus implied that they were not God's children. Then he outright said they were not the children of Abraham.

Once again, they protested. "We were not born of fornication; we have one Father: God."

Then Jesus brought the hammer down. "If God were your Father, you would love Me, for I proceeded forth and have come from God, for I have not even come on My own initiative, but He sent Me. Why do you not understand what I am saying? It is because you cannot hear My word."

Can you sense Jesus' frustration with them? They went back and forth with this argument about whether or not they knew God. And then Jesus really set them straight:

"You are of your father the devil, and you want to do the desires of your father. He was a murderer from the beginning, and does not stand in the truth because there is no truth in him. Whenever he speaks a lie, he speaks from his own nature, for he is a liar and the father of lies. But because I speak the truth, you do not believe Me. Which one of you convicts Me of sin? If I speak truth, why do you not believe Me? He who is of God hears the words of God; for this reason you do not hear them, because you are not of God."

The audacity of Jesus' words is astounding. He acknowledged their connection to Abraham, then he told them that their father was not God but the devil. To the Jewish mind, this was not merely offensive; it was heresy. Jesus' assertion was also fatal to the idea that DNA determines whether or not God has chosen someone. The people could not simultaneously be God's chosen ones and the devil's children, could they?

Obviously upset, they responded with an accusation equally as harsh: "Do we not say rightly that You are a Samaritan and have a demon?"

The Samaritans were mongrels not allowed to worship in Jerusalem. The chosen ones fervently held that those mixed-race converts to Judaism were not "chosen." That's also why Jesus' parable of the good Samaritan was so offensive. Jesus, they charged, was not only an outcast, but one controlled by an evil spirit.

Jesus answered, "I do not have a demon; but I honor My Father, and you dishonor Me. But I do not seek My glory; there is One who seeks and judges. Truly, truly, I say to you, if anyone keeps My word he will never see death."

Now Jesus was offering something no human could provide: victory over death. When he spoke of his father, they probably assumed he spoke of Joseph, so they didn't yet connect that divine claim, but they understood this talk of never seeing death—and rejected it.

The Jews said to him, "Now we know that You have a demon. Abraham died, and the prophets also; and You say, 'If anyone keeps My word, he will never taste of death.' Surely You are not greater than our father Abraham, who died? The prophets died too; whom do You make Yourself out to be?"

Given the events of the time, we have to consider why the Jewish leaders were even listening to Jesus. He wasn't the first to claim special status. Many false messiahs had come and gone before him. Messianic cults existed, and the leaders of the synagogues knew these stories. They had a legitimate reason to test Jesus to determine who he was.

They couldn't write him off as a common lunatic; he had performed too many undisputed miracles. They couldn't write him off as a secular con artist; he had spoken with great authority regarding the law. He had power and knowledge, but he was also claiming that he knew God and that they—God's chosen people—did not. Clearly, in their minds, he was influenced by demons.

Jesus answered, "If I glorify Myself, My glory is nothing; it is My Father who glorifies Me, of whom you say, 'He is our God'; and you have not come to know Him, but I know Him; and if I say that I do not know Him, I will be a liar like you, but I do know Him and keep His word. Your father Abraham rejoiced to see My day, and he saw it and was glad."

If those who rejected Jesus weren't sure about him yet, they were now. He had to be insane. Who would claim to know their "father" Abraham? They said to him, "You are not yet fifty years old, and have You seen Abraham?"

Jesus replied, "Truly, truly, I say to you, before Abraham was born, I am" (John 8:33–59).

This was the last straw. His words, "I am," were not lost on these Jewish scholars. They understood this reference to God's divine name, which the law prohibited them from speaking. It also reminded them of the burning bush where Moses asked how he was to present God to the enslaved Israelites in Egypt. God had said to Moses, "Thus you shall say to the sons of Israel, 'I AM has sent me to you'" (Ex. 3:14).

Jesus now claimed this divinity, so they deemed him a heretic. According to their law, which God had given them, Jesus of Nazareth was worthy of death. They started gathering up stones to carry out justice, but Jesus hid from them and left the temple.

By speaking to the Jews, Jesus fulfilled his promise to bring the gospel of salvation through faith to the chosen people first. He sent his disciples exclusively to evangelize the descendants of Jacob. As he approached Jerusalem one last time, though, knowing that his crucifixion was near, many Gentiles in the crowd sought him out.

They approached Philip saying, "Sir, we wish to see Jesus."

When the disciples reported this to Jesus, he said,

"The hour has come for the Son of Man to be glorified. Truly, truly, I say to you, unless a grain of wheat falls into the earth and dies, it remains alone; but if it dies, it bears much fruit. He who loves his life loses it, and he who hates his life in this world will keep it to life eternal. If anyone serves Me, he must follow Me; and where I am, there My servant will be also; if anyone serves Me, the Father will honor him." (John 12:23–26)

In addition to foretelling his death, Jesus was acknowledging how faith precluded birthright. Jacob, the second son, had taken the family blessing from his older brother, Esau. Later, Jacob blessed the second of Joseph's sons, Ephraim. Now, Jesus was blessing the second sons of the greater world, soon to be called Christians. The necessary traits of God's chosen people were changing.

Into All the Earth

After his death and resurrection, Christ appeared to his disciples and announced, "All authority has been given to Me in heaven and on earth." The spiritual and earthly authority that had once resided in the temple, the law, the ark, and the chosen people now resided exclusively and fully in Jesus Christ. "Go therefore and make disciples of all the nations, baptizing them in the name of the Father and the Son and the Holy Spirit, teaching them to observe all that I commanded you; and lo, I am with you always, even to the end of the age" (Matt. 28:18–20).

The age of a chosen race would end with the disciples' generation. Those who heard the gospel of Jesus Christ and recognized him as the Messiah from that point on would receive eternal life. Those who rejected him would face the judgment of which he warned. As in generations past, those who did not follow God, now revealed in his Son, would face calamity of apocalyptic proportions. This would come as soon as AD 70, when the Jews were massacred by the Roman army, Jerusalem was destroyed, and the temple was razed, just as Jesus prophesied on the Mount of Olives.

After his ascension, the apostles were left with a short timeline. When he initially sent them out, he warned that they would be persecuted in the synagogues, arrested, brought before the authorities, betrayed, and hated by many. Though they were sent initially to the Jews, Christ said their persecutions would happen "as a testimony to them and to the Gentiles" (Matt. 10:18). These things did not happen while Jesus still lived, but after his death and resurrection it wasn't long before his prophecies started coming true. The apostles possessed an urgency because Christ had also predicted, "You will not finish going through the cities of Israel until the Son of Man comes" (Matt. 10:23). This coming was a reference to the judgment that would fall on that generation.

With a renewed and expanded mission, the apostles set out to reach as many people as possible, both Jew and Gentile. This great evangelistic effort began with the explosive events at Pentecost. Believers were added to the fold daily. Peter and John were arrested but released. Miracles followed the apostles, and many more began to believe Jesus was the Christ. The apostles were arrested again, and this time an angel released them and sent them to preach in the temple again. They were apprehended, beaten, told not to speak of Jesus, and released.

More disciples were sent out to minister, including Stephen, who was stoned for preaching against the Jewish leaders who rejected Christ. Saul, who persecuted followers of Christ, was accosted by God on the road to Damascus and also began to follow Christ. Philip went on to minister to a court official of the Ethiopian queen, one of the first detailed accounts of a disciple preaching to a Gentile.

For some, though, it was still difficult to get outside the mind-set Jesus' Jewish disciples had been raised with regarding who was chosen and who was unclean. Simon Peter was staying in the seaside village of Joppa when he saw a vision of animals lowered to the ground on a large sheetlike object. A voice spoke to him, saying, "Get up, Peter, kill and eat!"

Peter, still mindful of Jewish law, objected saying, "By no means, Lord, for I have never eaten anything unholy and unclean."

The voice replied, "What God has cleansed, no longer consider unholy." This happened three times, and then the vision faded.

Peter was perplexed. Shortly after, two men appeared at his host's home. They had been sent by a Roman centurion named Cornelius. God had spoken to this man of faith and told him where to find Peter. The Roman's servants said, "Cornelius, a centurion, a righteous and God-fearing man well spoken of by the entire nation of the Jews, was divinely directed by a holy angel to send for you to come to his house and hear a message from you."

The next day, Peter and some believers from Joppa went with the Romans to Caesarea to visit Cornelius. Upon arriving, they found a great crowd waiting to hear Peter. Amazed, Peter said, "You yourselves know how unlawful it is for a man who is a Jew to associate with a foreigner or to visit him; and yet God has shown me that I should not call any man unholy or unclean. That is why I came without even raising any objection when I was sent for."

The Romans explained that God had ordained their meeting, and they eagerly awaited Peter's message to them. Peter began, "I most certainly understand now that God is not one to show partiality, but in every nation the man who fears Him and does what is right is welcome to Him." He began relating the life of Christ to them, and the Holy Spirit fell on the whole crowd. The Jews with Peter were amazed that God would do for these Gentiles what he had done for the Jews at Pentecost. They stayed in Caesarea for several days, and many new, non-Jewish believers were baptized.

When they went back to Jerusalem, the Jewish believers confronted them for fellowshipping with Gentiles. Peter explained his vision and the events in Caesarea. Then the believers in Jerusalem understood what was happening and joyfully said, "God has granted to the Gentiles also the repentance that leads to life" (Acts 10:1–11:18).

This revelation was an adjustment. A history of Jewish exclusiveness was consumed by the life of Christ and ministry of the Holy Spirit. The invitation to fellowship with God that had been enjoyed by generations of Jacob's descendants was now being extended to everyone. Christ had chosen not only Jews but Gentiles as well. All who believed in him would be blessed. The ranks of the chosen people were growing fast.

Paul's Mystery

As an expert on the Scriptures and the law, Paul wrestled with this transition from physical birthright to spiritual birthright. Having once persecuted and killed followers of Jesus, he understood that their teachings were radically different from Jewish law. Even after being transformed on the road to Damascus, he had to work out this new way of thinking. He called it a "mystery."

His letter "to all who are beloved of God in Rome, called as saints" dealt meticulously with this transition (Rom. 1:7). He argued that because of sin and unbelief, everyone needed a savior. While acknowledging the blessings that came through the line of Jacob, he asserted that they were the result of faith, not a matter of Jewish law. He made the startling statement, "For he is not a Jew who is one outwardly, nor is circumcision that which is outward in the flesh. But he is a Jew who is one inwardly; and circumcision is that which is of the heart, by the Spirit, not by the letter" (Rom. 2:28–29).

Paul further emphasized his point by asking, "Is God the God of Jews only? Is He not the God of Gentiles also?" To his question, he gave the clearest answer regarding the identity of God's people: "Yes, of Gentiles also, since indeed God who will justify the circumcised by faith and the uncircumcised through faith is one" (Rom. 3:29–30).

In perhaps the most concise passage on the very essence of salvation, Paul eloquently wrote,

If you confess with your mouth Jesus as Lord, and believe in your heart that God raised Him from the dead, you will be saved; for with the heart a person believes, resulting in righteousness, and with the mouth he confesses, resulting in salvation. For the Scripture says, "Whoever believes in Him will not be disappointed." For there is no distinction between Jew and Greek; for the same Lord is Lord of all, abounding in riches for all who call on Him; for "whoever will call on the name of the Lord will be saved." (Rom. 10:9–13)

He used the illustration of a widow who had remarried. Since her former husband was dead, he argued, she would not be an adulteress for marrying another man. Likewise, the law was dead, and God's people would be joined to another: Christ. Unlike the generations of Israelites who were separated from God by their unbelief, Paul wrote, those who believed in Christ would not face the same fate: "For I am convinced that neither death, nor life, nor angels, nor principalities, nor things present, nor things to come, nor powers, nor height, nor depth, nor any other created thing, will be able to separate us from the love of God, which is in Christ Jesus our Lord" (Rom. 8:38–39).

He reiterated that being Jewish by birth was no longer the measure of God's favor:

> For they are not all Israel who are descended from Israel; nor are they all children because they are Abraham's descendants, but: "through Isaac your descendants will be named." That is, it is not the children of the flesh who are children of God, but the children of the promise are regarded as descendants. (Rom. 9:6–8)

Isaac symbolized the original promise made to Abraham that he would be the father of many nations. This came in the flesh, through a nation of people called Israelites. But since the promised Messiah had arrived, all who believed in Christ would be regarded as children of the promise, regardless of any fleshly connection of Isaac and Abraham. The new inheritance belonged to those connected by faith, not DNA.

Paul also cautioned the Romans against pride for being brought into God's favor. Though the Jews were enemies "from the standpoint of the gospel," they were also "beloved for the sake of the fathers" (Rom. 11:28). They were cut off from God for their unbelief but could easily be brought back in through Christ if they would receive him as their Messiah. The Israelites were not cast off and replaced by Gentiles; all those who believed in Jesus Christ, whether Jew or Gentile, became one family. Paul said this was "according to the revelation of the mystery which has been kept secret for long ages past, but now is manifested" and "made known to all the nations, leading to obedience of faith" (Rom. 16:25–26). Obedience to the law routinely failed. With the arrival of the promised Messiah, Paul asserted, the only obedience that matters is faith in Christ.

Paul continued pressing this theme in his letters to believers throughout the land. He wrote to the believers in Ephesus that God "made known to us the mystery of His will" by "the summing up of all things in Christ." In him "we have obtained an inheritance . . . with a view to the redemption of God's own possession" (Eph. 1:9–14). This mystery, he explained, is "that the Gentiles are fellow heirs and fellow members of the body, and fellow partakers of the promise in Christ Jesus through the gospel" (Eph. 3:6).

To the church in Corinth, Paul referred to "those who are the called, both Jews and Greeks" (1 Cor. 1:24). He stated, "For by one Spirit we were all baptized into one body, whether Jews or Greeks, whether slaves or free, and we were all made to drink of one Spirit" (1 Cor. 12:13).

To the Colossian believers, he wrote about "the mystery which has been hidden from the past ages and generations, but has now been manifested to his saints, to whom God willed to make known what is the riches of the glory of this mystery among the Gentiles, which is Christ in you, the hope of glory" (Col. 1:26–27). He further shattered the barrier between Jews and Gentiles by pointedly stating, "There is no distinction between Greek and Jew, circumcised and uncircumcised, barbarian, Scythian, slave and freeman, but Christ is all, and in all." His very next statement was addressed to "those who have been chosen of God" (Col. 3:11–12).

Again, he said to believers in Galatia, "For you are all sons of God through faith in Christ Jesus. For all of you who were baptized into Christ have clothed yourselves with Christ. There is neither Jew nor Greek, there is neither slave nor free man, there is neither male nor female; for you are all one in Christ Jesus. And if you belong to Christ, then you are Abraham's descendants, heirs according to promise" (Gal. 3:26–29).

Today's Chosen

People still argue today about whom God has chosen. It is a race, some say. Others contend it is their particular denomination or sect. Many Christ followers even hold to the Old Testament notion that the descendants of Jacob are God's chosen people, separate from Christians. While overlooking the complexities of genealogy, they transfer the conditional, fleshly promises made to Abraham and Jacob to those living in the contemporary, reconstituted state of Israel. But even Jewish scholars debate what makes a Jew today. Is it genetic, or is it spiritual? If it is genetic, then what percentage qualifies?

Given that the Jacobites are what geneticists consider a "founding group" within the Jewish people, there is likely an artifact of Israelite DNA in an astounding number of people today. If you go back ten generations, or about 350 years, everyone has a potential 1,024 contributors to his or her genetic makeup (two parents, four grand-parents, eight great-grandparents, and so on). If you go back twenty generations, or about seven hundred years, it jumps to more than a million. And if you go back thirty generations, or about 1,050 years, it explodes to more than a billion people. Of course, marriage among cousins reduces the number, but the shuffling of the gene pool over so many years makes it difficult to pinpoint exact lineage. Historians and theologians generally place the beginning of the twelve tribes of Israel at about four thousand years ago, so you can imagine the diffi-culty in tracing them to modern times.

Compounding the issue are contractions in the gene pool through wars and targeted slaughter, dilution through generations of inter-marriage, and the scattering of the gene pool through multiple diaspora. The so-called lost tribes of Israel, which constituted an estimated 90 percent of the original population, further confuse the story. Wild speculation of their fate has led to an array of claims over the centuries.

In the early 1500s, Bartolomé de Las Casas, a Spanish man from a wealthy family, traveled to New Spain (mainly in the Caribbean and South America) to help protect Native Americans in Spanish colonies. Known as the Defender of the Indians, his training as a priest com-pelled him to protest the slaughter and enslavement of these people. He promoted the idea that the indigenous peoples were descendants of the "lost tribes" and deserved to be treated with the respect accorded to the Israelites.[1]

In the mid-1600s, a Portuguese-born rabbi named Menasseh ben Israel lobbied England's Lord Protectorate Oliver Cromwell to allow Jews to be English citizens. They had been banned since 1290, but ben Israel convinced many English leaders that in order for a Jewish mes-siah to return, Jewish enclaves had to be established in all parts of the earth. Though he didn't get everything he wished, the Cromwellian

Protectorate of 1656 revoked the ban and allowed Jews to flourish in England. In his 1650 book, *The Hope of Israel*, ben Israel argued that first inhabitants of the Americas were "white and bearded" and "at this day they keep the Jewish Religion." In order to fulfill prophecy, he said they would need to return to the land of Israel.[2]

Many abolitionists in the early 1800s believed that the second coming of Christ would be ushered in by converting Native Americans to Christianity and freeing the African slaves. Joseph Smith, founder of Mormonism, believed the Native Americans were descendants of a lost Israelite tribe called Lamanites. Proselytizing the Natives was an important mission for the early Mormons. Their book *Doctrine and Covenants* says, "But before the great day of the Lord shall come, Jacob shall flourish in the wilderness, and the Lamanites shall blossom as the rose."[3]

Herbert W. Armstrong, founder of the Worldwide Church of God in 1933, promoted the idea that whites from Europe were long-lost tribes—and not just any tribes, but the only ones who would be blessed by God. In his 1945 book *The United States and Britain in Prophecy*, released to usher in the end-times, he claimed that the tribe of Dan named the Danube River and Denmark. He also wrote,

> The people of the house of Israel also migrated northwest across Europe. But they did not stop in Germany. They continued on farther west and north—into Western Europe—France, Belgium, Holland, the Scandinavian countries, and the British Isles—where they are to this day, except for the tribe of Manasseh, which much later migrated to North America and became the United States.[4]

In 1953, American writer Nathan Ausubel published his *Pictorial History of the Jewish People.* He connected various groups to the lost tribes, including some in Iraq, Iran, Yemen, Georgia, Afghanistan, China, Egypt, Tunisia, Ethiopia, Morocco, and Algeria.

In 1975, Israel's chief rabbis recognized the Falasha tribe of Ethiopia as the lost descendants of the tribe of Dan. A quarter of a century later, DNA evidence contradicted their claim. They are now believed to be one of the few tribes that remained faithful to ancient converts.[5]

In 1980, Joseph Eidelberg published *The Japanese and the Lost Tribes of Israel* in which he analyzed ancient traditions, religious ceremonies, historical names, haiku poetry, folk songs, and language to conclude that the Japanese were a lost tribe.

Today, Nigeria's Igbo tribe claims to be from the tribes of Naphtali, Gad, Manasseh, Ephraim, Zebulun, or Levi. A large group of Pashtun clans in Afghanistan and Pakistan call themselves *Yousafzai*, which means "Sons of Joseph," raising the peculiar and troubling question of whether Muslim fundamentalists who seek to wipe out all Jews could bear DNA from the original twelve tribes. The Chiang Min people in northwest China claim Jewish roots as well. The Lemda people of Zimbabwe and South Africa practice many Jewish-style customs and pray in a language that is a mix of Hebrew and Arabic. Unlike most other claimants, the Lemda have shown a remarkable rate of DNA matches to assumed Jewish genetic markers.

There is even a debate over the ancestry of England's Prince William and Kate Middleton, the Duke and Duchess of Cambridge and heirs to the royal throne. Some claim Kate's mother is Jewish, which would make the duchess Jewish according to Jewish tradition and law. Some also speculate that Princess Diana was Jewish, which would make the duke Jewish as well. In an odd agreement between Zionist advocates who want a Jewish throne in London and anti-Semites who fear a Jewish takeover of the world, there is ample breath given to this idea of Judaism at Buckingham Palace. There are also many who debunk the notion, but one thing is clear: despite the long and horrific history of Jewish persecution, people are lining up to claim the blessings of Jacob.

Modern Jews

So what about the Jewish people today? Most American Jews are Ashkenazic, or Germanic, largely from those who emigrated from Germany and Eastern Europe from the mid-1800s to the early 1900s. Recent research concludes that they come from a "bottleneck" of about 350 individuals from around AD 1300 who were half European and half Middle Eastern. Mitochondrial DNA, which is passed on exclusively from mother to child, suggests that most Ashkenazim were converts to Judaism, not descendants of Jacob.[6]

Sephardic Jews are mainly from Spain, Portugal, North Africa, and the Middle East. Jewish DNA can be found in Hispanics of New Mexico, because many Jews went to Spain to avoid persecution, then fled Europe during the Inquisition. Of course, most New Mexicans also have Spanish and Native American genes as well.

Most Jews living in modern Israel are believed to be Ashkenazic descendants of Jews from France, Germany, and Eastern Europe. Of course, there is much debate over who is genetically linked to the original twelve tribes. It's a messy and divisive subject among scientists and religious leaders.

Genetically speaking, traces of Jewish genes are found heavily in Eastern Europe, India, and all over the Middle East. A remnant of fairly pure Samaritans live near Tel Aviv today, still believing they are the true chosen people, adhering more closely to the teachings of Moses than most Israelis.

As mentioned earlier, Jewish tradition and law states that if a mother is Jewish, her children are Jewish regardless of the father's ancestry. Tribal affiliation was a matter of the father, but Jewish tradition still holds to the mother. Hypothetically, a man with a Jewish woman five generations back on his maternal line would be considered Jewish even if the rest of his ancestors were Arab. He would be 97 percent Arab genetically, but Jewish by tradition. The modern state of Israel welcomes all who identify themselves as Jews, whether by blood or conversion. That is perfectly within their rights as a modern nation, but that should not be confused with any measure of genetic purity.

If Jewishness is determined by faith, then anyone who converts can call him- or herself a Jew. Still, all this raises the question of whether God sees genes, faith, or national law. According to the Bible, only faith matters. Though controversial when Jesus spoke about it and divisive when Paul wrote about it, the idea of faith as the indicator of God's favor has existed since the old covenant. The prophets foresaw it, and the stories of Rahab and Ruth exemplified it. Christ just brought it to fruition because he is the one in whom our faith must be placed to break every curse and unleash God's blessings. But it's not faith in the old covenant or Jewish law that leads us to the promise of being chosen people; it's faith in Jesus Christ.

Living the Promise

We are, as Paul wrote, "vessels of mercy, which He prepared beforehand for glory, even us, whom He also called, not from among Jews only, but also from among Gentiles" (Rom. 9:23–24). Whether we have any Jewish DNA doesn't matter. The emphasis for Christians today should be the same as it was in the apostles' time: preaching the one, singular gospel to all the world, both Jewish and Gentile. Jesus Christ died to save all people. God loves all people fully. The Holy Spirit dwells in all believers in the same manner. The old heaven and earth structure has passed away, and the new authority resides in Christ and his representatives on earth.

Can there really be any argument about who is now chosen, or set apart, by God? If the New Testament maintains any credibility, then we can only say that God's people are those who believe in God's Chosen One, Jesus Christ. Our DNA tells an ethnic tale, but whether Irish or Indian, American or Angolan, Chinese or Chilean, Syrian or South African, our natural traits are swallowed up in our supernatural identity.

Jesus is not a polygamist. He has only one bride. Any other claim is purely religious. It is an artifact of a time that is past. Rather than dwell in the shadows of the past, we must step into the light of today's truth: all believers are one in Christ, "chosen of God, holy and beloved" (Col. 3:12). This is the promise of the chosen people. All who come to Christ are made one, set apart for his purpose and blessed as sons and daughters.

CHAPTER 5

The Promise of the Priest

"You shall be to Me a kingdom of priests."
EXODUS 19:6

Most Protestant Christians are aware of the priesthood but largely dismiss it as an Old Testament thing or a Catholic thing. In the more fundamentalist churches I've visited, where Catholicism is demonized and even called "the whore of Babylon" of Revelation, just discussing the idea of a priest in a positive light can get you in trouble. Aside from that bit of eschatology being a terrible misrepresentation of the original text, failure to grasp God's purpose of the priesthood and how it was gloriously transformed by Christ—when he both fulfilled it and transferred it to his followers—results in a missed opportunity to fill the roles for which God ordained us. The promise of the priest qualifies otherwise unqualified people to participate actively in his kingdom, expanding his influence and impacting people's lives.

In the book of Hebrews, the writer explained to the Jewish people the relationship between Jesus Christ and the priesthood. Because of the readers' history and familiarity with the roles of the high priest and the lesser priests, they understood how it related to their lives under the new covenant. But Christians in the twenty-first century largely miss the significance of the priesthood, the role of Christ as the High Priest, and us as modern-day priests.

This sacred order of ministers holds multiple promises. Christ as High Priest grants us privileges beyond anything the Israelites experienced. A priestly role empowers us to live beyond our natural abilities, and the responsibilities entrusted to the priesthood outline a way of living that ushers in the presence of God.

To understand God's plan for the priesthood, we must look to the beginning, even before the formal inauguration of the Levitical dynasty. Once we understand the purpose and history of the old priesthood, we can better grasp and appreciate how it relates to us today.

Origin of the Priesthood

In the beginning, every man served in his own priestly role. He made sacrifices for his sin, offered gifts to his Creator, and sought divine instruction for himself. In the days of Noah, Abraham, Jacob, and Job, these duties fell to the head of household, with the firstborn son of each household inheriting the priestly office. The first mention of a designated priest is Melchizedek, a mysterious "king of Salem" who was said to have had no father or mother. (Whether figurative or literal, we do not know. More about this fascinating figure later.)

Later on, when God led his people out of slavery in Egypt, he appointed Moses as their leader and intermediary to God as he delivered them from the oppression of Pharaoh. God initiated his covenant when he said, through Moses,

> "'Now if you obey me fully and keep my covenant, then out of all nations you will be my treasured possession. Although the whole earth is mine, you will be for me a kingdom of priests and a holy nation.' These are the words you are to speak to the Israelites." (Ex. 19:5–6 NIV)

While Moses ascended the mountain of God to experience his holy presence and receive laws for peaceful, prosperous living, the people were warned to stay behind, lest they be destroyed. Because of their sins, they could not approach the powerful presence of the holy God. Moses' interactions with God set the stage for a pattern that continued throughout the Old Testament. Only the elect could enter into the presence of God. The common, sinful man, even if a part of God's chosen people, could not approach a holy God.

Remember when Moses descended the mountain with the Ten Commandments and he found the people worshipping a golden calf? When he called forward those who would stand with him against this evil, only one tribe answered the call: the Levites. So Moses ordered them to kill those engaged in the ritual and went back to Sinai to beg for God's mercy. Soon after, God gave more laws for his lawless people, part of which established the priesthood.

At that point, the priesthood of the populace was gone. Only the Levites were ordained in the priestly role. They served as the foundation for a perpetual priesthood as the duties passed down through generations of their tribe alone.

Levi served as high priest, and his sons Gershon, Kohath, and Merari were assigned specific supporting roles. From the sons came generations of three levels of service. Kohath's grandson Aaron formed the core of the priesthood. Kohath's other descendants (not from Aaron) were given charge of the most sacred portions of the tabernacle, including the ark, the lampstand, and the altar. The descendants of Gershon and Merari were assigned lesser duties, including the screens and hangings and care of the pillars around the court, respectively. As the people followed the presence of God in a cloud by day and a pillar of fire by night, the three Levitical clans assembled, disassembled, and cared for the tabernacle, sanctuary, and courts.

Upon Aaron's death, the duties of high priest went, as instructed by God, to the oldest surviving son, provided he did not have a physical defect. Eleazar assumed the duties, and his descendants continued the tradition until the time of King Saul, when Eli, a descendant of Eleazar's brother Ithamar, assumed office. Under King Solomon, the Aaronic line was restored when Zadok took the place of Eli's descendant, Abiathar. The phrase "line of Zadok" is also used to represent the original line of priests through Aaron.

God's instructions for the priests' activities were very specific. He told them exactly how to build the temple (even when moving around in the wilderness), how to act, how to dress, what to eat, and so on. The early rituals included extensive purification rites, communion, and blood sacrifice.

The core purpose of the priesthood was to reestablish a relationship between Holy God and sinful man. Ever since the fall in the garden of Eden, sin had created a chasm. Still, God sought fellowship with his people and pursued a covenant relationship with them. The priestly tradition continued until Aristobulus was executed by Herod in 35 BC. After that, the high priests were appointed by Rome. With Aristobulus's death, the bloodline of the priests ended, but God's purpose did not.

Priests of Darkness

When Jesus entered the scene, the Levitical priesthood was gone. The high priest was not a descendent of Aaron, and the original purpose of the priests was lost in a web of legalism. Most crucial, there was scant relationship between the priests and the true God.

The words of the prophet Hosea had come true:

> Because you have rejected knowledge,
> I also will reject you from being My priest.
> Since you have forgotten the law of your God,
> I also will forget your children.
> The more they multiplied, the more they sinned against Me;
> I will change their glory into shame. (Hos. 4:6–7)

Jesus condemned those who had assumed the roles of the priests in his day, and they were numerous. How numerous? Here's an outline of the priesthood then: The high priest during Christ's ministry was Joseph Caiaphas. His father-in-law, Annas, preceded him in the office and still held considerable power, which is why Jesus was first sent to Annas and then to Caiaphas before being crucified. Both were Sadducees, a sect tied to the line of Zadok. There were about two hundred highborn Jews serving under Caiaphas as chief priests; they wielded great influence with their Roman procurators. Then there were thousands of ordinary priests across the region, carrying out temple duties in rotations. Finally, there were almost ten thousand Levites sharing duties ranging from temple guards to ceremony preparation.

Thrown into this mix were the Pharisees, who were not technically priests but held great influence during the time of Christ. They had strong differences with the Sadducees regarding written law versus oral law, attitudes toward the Romans, and theology of things such as free will and the afterlife.

Jesus didn't get along with any of them very well. "The scribes and the Pharisees have seated themselves in the chair of Moses; therefore all that they tell you, do and observe, but do not do according to their deeds; for they say things and do not do them" (Matt. 23:2–3).

You can imagine how well that went over with them. Here was the one claiming to be not just a prophet but the incarnate Son of God, able to forgive sin, perform miracles, and talk to God, yet he did not show them the respect they felt was bestowed on them by tradition and the law. Jesus called them fools, blind guides, hypocrites, and snakes. They thought he was a heretic.

Jesus proclaimed the departure of God's blessing on the priesthood when he said, "Behold, your house is being left to you desolate! For I say to you, from now on you will not see Me until you say, 'Blessed is He who comes in the name of the Lord!'" (Matt. 23:38–39).

Why would Jesus so aggressively and abrasively disrupt what God had instituted? Maybe it was because the priesthood had failed in every capacity. Specifically, under Caiaphas it had prostituted itself to Rome. Generally, it had, as Hosea noted, exchanged the glory of God for a disgraceful symbol of status, taking pride in the law rather than the Lawgiver.

Interestingly, during the Last Supper, Jesus wore a simple, seamless white tunic, the very garment prescribed by God for the high priest to wear on the Day of Atonement. He was assuming the role of the high priest as he performed the final sacrifice for the sin of the world. In doing so, he rewrote the terms of the priesthood, returning it to the populace and laying the foundation for a new relationship between God and man—one that directly affects the way you and I approach God and the world today.

A Higher Priest

How did Christ have the authority to change the law given by God at Sinai regarding the priesthood? The Bible names one priest who predates and supersedes the Levitical line. That is a mysterious figure called Melchizedek, whose name means "king of righteousness." He appears in Genesis 14:18–20:

> Melchizedek king of Salem brought out bread and wine; now he was a priest of God Most High. He blessed him and said,
>
> "Blessed be Abram of God Most High,
> Possessor of heaven and earth;
> And blessed be God Most High,
> Who has delivered your enemies into your hand."
> He [Abram] gave him a tenth of all.

Abraham (still called "Abram" at the time of the encounter) honored and submitted to Melchizedek's authority by tithing to him. The tithe indicates Abraham's recognition of the priest's position and authority. Melchizedek is identified as both king of Salem, which became Jerusalem, and a priest of God Most High. Further identification remains difficult. Some believe that Melchizedek was Shem, the son of Noah. However, the writer of Hebrews referred to Melchizedek as one "without father, without mother, without genealogy, having neither beginning of days nor end of life" (7:3). Many theologians speculate that Melchizedek was actually Jesus Christ preincarnate. Some even believe that Melchizedek was an angel on the order of Michael or Gabriel. However, the fact that Melchizedek was the king of an earthly city tends to point to an actual man of flesh and blood.

The important thing about Melchizedek is not what we don't

know, but what we do know, specifically, that Melchizedek was a shadow of the Messiah. He represented an authority higher than Levi's or Aaron's descendants. The writer of Hebrews explained how Jesus Christ fulfilled the line of priests and assumed the superior and eternal order of Melchizedek:

> Now if perfection was through the Levitical priesthood (for on the basis of it the people received the Law), what further need was there for another priest to arise according to the order of Melchizedek, and not be designated according to the order of Aaron? For when the priesthood is changed, of necessity there takes place a change of law also. For the one concerning whom these things are spoken belongs to another tribe, from which no one has officiated at the altar. For it is evident that our Lord was descended from Judah, a tribe with reference to which Moses spoke nothing concerning priests. And this is clearer still, if another priest arises according to the likeness of Melchizedek, who has become such not on the basis of a law of physical requirement, but according to the power of an indestructible life. For it is attested of Him, "You are a priest *forever* according to the order of Melchizedek." (7:11–17, emphasis added)

Beyond fulfilling the purpose of the priesthood, Jesus descended from an authority even higher than that of Aaron's line. Because the Levitical line was so polluted, it was necessary for Jesus to rise above the earthly line and affirm his superior position.

> For, on the one hand, there is a setting aside of a former commandment because of its weakness and uselessness (for the Law made nothing perfect), and on the other hand there is a bringing

in of a better hope, through which we draw near to God. And inasmuch as it was not without an oath (for they indeed became priests without an oath, but He with an oath through the One who said to Him,

"The Lord has sworn

And will not change His mind,

'You are a priest forever'");

so much the more also Jesus has become the guarantee of a better covenant. (Heb. 7:18–22)

The ability for man to relate to God was finalized once and for all through a heavenly priest who offered something better than any earthly priest could. The chosen people had failed to uphold the old covenant, but God still delivered the promised Messiah. Through him, a better covenant came into being and exists eternally because Jesus Christ lives forever. It is through the hope of Christ, the eternal High Priest, that we draw near to God.

The former priests, on the one hand, existed in greater numbers because they were prevented by death from continuing, but Jesus, on the other hand, because He continues forever, holds His priesthood permanently. Therefore He is able also to save forever those who draw near to God through Him, since He always lives to make intercession for them.

For it was fitting for us to have such a high priest, holy, innocent, undefiled, separated from sinners and exalted above the heavens; who does not need daily, like those high priests, to offer up sacrifices, first for His own sins and then for the sins of the people, because this He did once for all when He offered up Himself. For the Law appoints men as high priests who are weak, but the word of the oath, which came after the Law, appoints a Son, made perfect forever. (Heb. 7:23–28)

The ramifications of this declaration are staggering! In the same way that Jesus did not come to abolish the law but to fulfill it, he also came to rescue and complete the priestly line. Jesus Christ took over the role of High Priest once and for all. All of the priestly functions now reside in the person of Christ. He atoned for our sins, gave the law under which we live, and provided the only way for sinful man to come to Holy God.

This is the fulfillment of the prophecy in Jeremiah 31, where God promised, "Behold, days are coming . . . when I will make a new covenant . . . and I will be their God, and they shall be My people" (vv. 31, 33). Jesus Christ is the "mediator of a better covenant, which has been enacted on better promises" (Heb. 8:6). The covenant is better for many reasons, one of which is the perfection of the High Priest who, unlike all of the Jewish high priests, cannot falter. This new covenant can never be broken.

Religion often attempts to reinvent and reincorporate the old-style priesthood. Judaism, of course, still functions under the Old Testament model, although without a temple it retains very little of the original office of Aaron. Non-Christian religions, and a few that call themselves Christian, sometimes follow the same concept of an intermediary who holds authority over other people and stands as the only way to a relationship with God. While it is perfectly appropriate for believers to help others in a priestly way, any imposition of authority that denies an intimate, direct connection with our heavenly Father falls short of new-covenant truth. The shadow priesthood disappeared forever when Jesus resurrected. Now we come directly into the inner courts and Holy of Holies because we serve the last High Priest, who reigns forever.

The Priesthood of the People

What does it mean for us to live now with a priesthood of the people? When Moses went up to Mount Sinai, God said, "You shall be to Me a kingdom of priests" (Ex. 19:6). He was speaking of the Israelites, but hundreds of years later, the apostle Peter applied this old-covenant proclamation to all believers under the new covenant, calling them a "royal priesthood." This means that the change in the priesthood through Christ has handed down some of its original functions to Christians today.

Let's focus on four purposes of the priesthood that carry over to this new age and that, under the High Priesthood of Christ, directly guide the steps of believers.

Representing God

Right after Peter called believers a "royal priesthood," he stated that the purpose is "so that you may proclaim the excellencies of Him who has called you out of darkness into His marvelous light" (1 Peter 2:9). What exactly does that mean?

For one, it contrasts darkness and light, blindness and sight. Metaphorically, it also represents knowledge and ignorance. That's the journey Christ takes us on. We're born asleep, but he wakes us up. We open our new eyes to see things as they really are. We gain understanding beyond the capabilities of our limited minds. This calling into the royal priesthood is—to break down the Greek word translated "marvelous"—amazing, wonderful, extraordinary, and passing human comprehension.

We are allowed to walk this amazing, wonderful, extraordinary path because we are "called." That word can also be translated "invited." It is an invitation to everyone, because God "desires all men to be saved and to come to the knowledge of the truth" (1 Tim. 2:4). But an invitation is not a summons; people are not forced to accept. God calls, but it's up to each person to answer. By demonstrating our transformation upon accepting this invitation, we extend his call to them. In a sense, we're telling people about the greatest party to ever take place and giving them a personalized invitation to join us. (That's an entirely different approach to standing on a sidewalk and screaming that people are going to hell. But I digress.)

Who has extended this invitation? Jesus Christ, of course. Our eternal High Priest. The one whose "excellencies" impart a better way of thought, feeling, and action. He is good, morally excellent, and pure. Through him, we experience these qualities. Anyone who has ever felt rotten, worthless, and dirty can appreciate the contrast he offers. To reflect Christ is not to heap guilt, condemnation, and judgment on others. It is simply to extol his excellence.

Note the verb used to kick off this whole mission: *proclaim*. We don't whisper it. We don't confine it to church buildings on Sunday morning. A proclamation is declared abroad, published for all to read, and spoken loud enough that anyone can hear it.

It has been said that our lives may be the only Bible some people ever read. Whether we like it or not, when we claim the name of Christ, people look for his reflection in us. While this may sound like bad news (and it would be if we were left to represent him in our own power), it comes with a promise. Jesus said, "If I am lifted up from the earth, [I] will draw all men to Myself" (John 12:32). He said this while foretelling his crucifixion, but the principle remains. If we simply lift him up—in our triumphs, failures, and everyday life—he will draw people to himself.

We need not fear imperfection. It's actually guaranteed, so why be shocked or discouraged by it? We simply need to repent of it, allow it to be a cause for spiritual growth, and continue the maturing process.

It's okay to admit our imperfections as long as we point to the One who is perfect. I believe that's why Jesus went after the Pharisees so directly. They held themselves up as the pious ones, praying, "God, I thank You that I am not like other people" (Luke 18:11). That's a dangerous representation of God, because when we fail, we project a flawed God to the world. When we confess our weaknesses and proclaim him as our strength, we bypass our faults and exalt the Forgiver.

The best way to represent him is simply to present him. A pretense of perfection focuses on the wrong place (on us) when we are called to the priestly role of publicly focusing on him.

Teaching Others

Next, as a priesthood, we are to teach and instruct people in the thoughts and ways of God. This, obviously, requires us to first know the thoughts and ways of God. But is that even possible?

Paul addressed this when writing to the church in Corinth, first by pointing out that the rulers of his age lacked wisdom and understanding. He condemned their ignorance by saying, "The thoughts of God no one knows except the Spirit of God" (1 Cor. 2:11). But then he went on to offer hope that we can come to know his mind:

> But a natural man does not accept the things of the Spirit of God, for they are foolishness to him; and he cannot understand them, because they are spiritually appraised. But he who is spiritual appraises all things, yet he himself is appraised by no one. For who has known the mind of the Lord, that he will instruct Him? But we have the mind of Christ. (1 Cor. 2:14–16)

It is a great New Testament blessing that mere mortals can know the thoughts of God. This is only possible when we have "the mind of Christ." Then and only then can we help others to know God's truth. On our own, the "natural man" cannot make sense of God's thoughts. Such limitations got Job in trouble with God when he questioned his goodness, power, and wisdom:

> Who is this that darkens counsel
> By words without knowledge?
> Now gird up your loins like a man,
> And I will ask you, and you instruct Me!
> Where were you when I laid the foundation of the earth?
> Tell Me, if you have understanding,
> Who set its measurements? Since you know.
> Or who stretched the line on it? (Job 38:2–5)

Job personified that gap between the natural man and God. Christ bridged that gap. On our own, we can't understand his ways. But when we are renewed daily through his Word and guided by the Holy Spirit, we can know his higher thoughts and impart his higher ways to others.

Part of the old priestly duties involved spotting blemishes, infections, and disease because they were the gatekeepers who kept impurities out of the temple. Today's believers must discern the rotten things of the world that seek to destroy us and keep us out of God's presence. The responsibility of knowing God's thoughts and ways is pointing out things that are not of God, the impurities that keep people apart from him.

Pop culture demands we call all things pure, even when they are not. We are labeled bigots, homophobes, misogynists, and worse simply because we see a blemish or disease and call it what it is. But in our roles as priests, we must have the courage and wisdom to speak the truth in love with the purpose of redemption for those afflicted with ungodly beliefs. Perhaps one of the most damning statements in the New Testament is Paul's opening to the Roman church when he called out those who know those things that God condemns, yet "not only continue to do these very things but also approve of those who practice them" (Rom. 1:32 NIV). We must never disgrace God's Word by hiding the truth about sin. It only serves to hurt us and those we should be helping.

At the same time, the goal must always be the salvation of sinners, never the destruction. This requires the ability to approach their imperfections without being stained by their sins, and the spiritual strength and maturity to shine his light into their darkness.

During an interview with A. R. Bernard, the brilliant pastor of Christian Cultural Center in Brooklyn, New York, he said to me, "Grace and truth came by Jesus Christ. Grace is God's extended mercy, [which] allows him to bypass his moral standards and go into the human condition for the purpose of bringing change. But it's only truth that brings the conviction necessary for change." This is the balance when we align ourselves with the mind of Christ. Grace gets us into the sinners' world; truth brings them out.

Leading Worship

Another duty of Old Testament priests was leading worship. When we think of leading worship, we imagine someone standing on a stage in church and singing hymns or worship songs. Certainly this is one aspect, but it just scratches the surface. As one who frequently stands on a church stage singing or playing in a worship band, I can tell you it is possible for both the musicians and the congregation to go through an entire set without really engaging in worship. Worship goes far beyond singing a song. It permeates everything we do, especially off the stage and outside of the church building.

The Hebrew and Greek words[1] translated "worship" in both Testaments imply much more than singing. One facet of meaning points to the act of bowing down. It carries both a spiritual and physical posture. "Come, let us worship and bow down," King David wrote. "Let us kneel before the LORD our Maker" (Ps. 95:6). Throughout the book of Revelation, people of God fall to their knees in worship. It's a natural response to an encounter with the Creator of the universe. The man or woman who has no sense of astonishment, reverence, respect, or overwhelming power simply has not experienced God.

Imagine looking out your window and seeing someone blown off their feet by a gust of wind. You'd think, *Wow, it's really windy!* (Or if you live in my region, you'd think, *Tornado!*) When we maintain a posture of genuine submission to the Lord in our attitudes and approaches with others, we point them to that Someone who is bigger than us. We make others want to find out what it's all about. We lead them to adopt a spirit of worship for themselves.

The other facet of worship described by the words used in the Bible means "serving."[2] The Greek includes the idea of work for hire. In a sense, when we become followers of Christ, enter into his priesthood, and assume priestly duties in the modern age, we're hired to serve God in any way he desires. And believe me, the pay is great and the benefits are even better!

"I urge you, brethren," Paul wrote, "by the mercies of God, to present your bodies a living and holy sacrifice, acceptable to God, which is your spiritual service of worship" (Rom. 12:1). We worship by giving ourselves completely to his purpose. This doesn't mean selling everything we own and moving to Congo. Well, okay it might. But for most people, it's not that cliché. It means hearing and obeying God's voice as much as possible. It means our Sunday morning worship is as active on Monday morning at work and Friday night on the town.

Believers must set an example, both for other believers and those who do not know Christ. This part of leading worship truly is leading, is being out front. We may have to blaze new trails among our peers, but that's what being a leader is all about. The idea of "leading from behind" just means pushing others in the way we think they should go. The problem is that nobody likes a pushy person, especially a pushy *religious* person. Worship leading means selling out to God even when nobody else does. It means walking that narrow, unpopular path in pursuit of his will and never looking back to see if anyone is behind you. You're setting an example and forging ahead with everything you have in obedience to God. That's true leadership and true worship.

Restoring the Fallen

The Old Testament priests offered sacrifices on behalf of people's sins, transgressions, and iniquities in order to restore their relationships with God. Fortunately, we don't have to do that anymore:

> But when Christ appeared as a high priest of the good things to come, He entered through the greater and more perfect tabernacle, not made with hands, that is to say, not of this creation; and not through the blood of goats and calves, but through His own blood, He entered the holy place once for all, having obtained eternal redemption. (Heb. 9:11–12)

In Christ, we have eternal redemption. The sacrificial blood of animals, which was a mere shadow of that which was obtained in Christ, has been made obsolete. No man can atone for the sins of another; only Christ can do that.

At the same time, we do have an obligation to help restore those who have fallen, assuming they want to be restored: "Brethren, even if anyone is caught in any trespass, you who are spiritual, restore such a one in a spirit of gentleness; each one looking to yourself, so that you too will not be tempted. Bear one another's burdens, and thereby fulfill the law of Christ" (Gal. 6:1–2). Paul wrote this to the church in Galatia. The principle stands today. For example, when a pastor confesses his infidelity, he should be removed from his position of authority but simultaneously brought back into accountability and fellowship if he will submit to those in spiritual authority. Note the spirit with which we should treat this type of person: gentleness. We've seen how harshly the world treats such a person. We don't need to do the same. We only need to look to our High Priest and emulate his attitude. "For we do not have a high priest who cannot sympathize with our weaknesses, but One who has been tempted in all things as we are, yet without sin. Therefore let us draw near with confidence to the throne of grace, so that we may receive mercy and find grace to help in time of need" (Heb. 4:15–16).

Think of someone caught in trespass, which is intentional wrong-doing. Was he or she treated gently and given grace and mercy? Usually not. Of course, if that person refuses to repent or submit, there comes a time of disassociation. When Paul ran up against such immorality in the Corinthian church, he said, "I have decided to deliver such a one to Satan for the destruction of his flesh, so that his spirit may be saved in the day of the Lord Jesus" (1 Cor. 5:5). If the trespasser repents, show mercy and grace. If he or she remains defiant, it may be necessary to release that person to the consequences of sin. But even in this action is the goal of salvation. How much more should we seek the restoration of those who are repentant? This is how we should approach such situations.

To restore the fallen, we must be among those "who are spiritual."

That simply indicates we must live with a consistent level of wisdom, discernment, and maturity. There is no shortage of people who need to be restored, so it's important that we remain close to Christ to fulfill this priestly function entrusted to us.

Living the Promise

The priests of the Old Testament were flawed, yet they still served God by fulfilling their designated roles. Today, in this new era of authority, we serve God through the power that Jesus Christ imparts to us in the Holy Spirit. As a believer, you represent God by presenting and proclaiming his goodness to others. It's his perfection, not your effort, that draws people to him.

Believe the promise that he empowers you to inspire and encourage others when you simply obey him. Live each day with the confidence that you have been ordained by the Spirit to function in a priestly role, representing God, teaching others, leading worship, and restoring the fallen. This is your awesome privilege and responsibility, established from the beginning and operative to the end.

CHAPTER 6

The Promise of the Temple

The LORD is in His holy temple.
PSALM 11:4

If you've spent much time in church, then I am sure you've heard the same myth I did. As a child, I heard it hundreds of times growing up in a Southern Baptist church. Later, I heard it again in the United Methodist church in which my wife and I married, as well as a couple of nondenominational, charismatic-leaning churches we later attended. It's echoed in Christian music and pulpits across the world. "Welcome to the house of God, my friend," one popular song begins. Consistent among all Christian spaces is the thought that a church building is the dwelling place of God.

The Catholic Answers Forum makes this bold claim: "The Catholic Church is where God resides—we have Our Lord in the Blessed Sacrament 24 hours a day. The images, statues and paintings are a reminder of whose House this is."[1]

When I walked through the Buddhist temple Wat Phnom in Phnom Penh, Cambodia, I could tell that the monks and the visitors treated the place as sacred. As I stood shoeless watching people burn incense and kneel in reverence under the empty gaze of a giant gold statue of the Buddha, it felt more like a museum than a place to meet God. Sadly, many Christian churches feel the same.

In modern religion, I am continually amazed by the idea that a building can contain God. I realize that referring to a church, temple, cathedral, or other place of worship as the "house of God" is a colloquialism, but it is at best misleading and at worst wrong. The New Testament puts the dwelling place of God in two places (not simultaneously). Neither is a building.

The idea of God residing in something made of human hands is purely an Old Testament view, and an incomplete one at that. Yet many in our new-covenant age still hold to a form of the idea, clinging to the shadow despite living in the full light of day.

To understand this concept of a "house of God" as a physical building inhabited by a spiritual being, we must look to the original structural dwelling place of God: the tabernacle. When we follow it through history and understand the foundational shift that took place at the crucifixion, we find a promise greater than the idea that God dwells in a building.

Constructing the Temple

After delivering his people out of slavery in Egypt, the Lord instructed Moses to have the people "construct a sanctuary for Me, that I may dwell among them" (Ex. 25:8). He then gave complete instructions on building it, with exact measurements, colors, materials, and contents.

The tabernacle consisted of a 150-by-75-square-foot courtyard separated from the people by curtains and poles and containing a bronze altar and washing basin in the center. Behind the altar and basin stood a tent called the Tent of Meeting. Inside the Tent of Meeting was the Holy Place with a golden table, lampstand, and incense altar. Behind the furnishings was a curtain that separated the Holy of Holies where the ark of the covenant rested.

Once the Israelites obeyed God's instructions and built this sanctuary, God's presence lived among the people:

> Then the cloud covered the tent of meeting, and the glory of the LORD filled the tabernacle. Moses was not able to enter the tent of meeting because the cloud had settled on it, and the glory of the LORD filled the tabernacle. Throughout all their journeys whenever the cloud was taken up from over the tabernacle, the sons of Israel would set out; but if the cloud was not taken up, then they did not set out until the day when it was taken up. For throughout all their journeys, the cloud of the LORD was on the tabernacle by day, and there was fire in it by night, in the sight of all the house of Israel. (Ex. 40:34–38)

The tabernacle was the earthly structure where heavenly God dwelt. Only certain people—the priests—could enter it, and even they were restricted to certain parts at certain times after carrying out specific rites of sacrifice and cleansing. Straying from the exact instructions of the tabernacle resulted in death, as a result of the body of a sinful, unclean man being exposed to the overwhelming power of the pure, holy God. Like the devastating energy of a tidal wave or volcanic explosion, an unprepared man could not stand the awesome, raw power of God.

Under the reign of King David, plans were drawn up for a permanent building to replace the portable tabernacle. But because David was a man of war, he was not allowed to build the temple. The honor fell to his son, Solomon, who used more than 180,000 men over the course of seven years to complete the monumental task.

When Solomon completed the first temple, called Solomon's temple, the ark of the covenant and all of the tabernacle utensils were brought in. The cloud of God's presence appeared in the temple, and Solomon consecrated what he called "a place for Your dwelling forever" (1 Kings 8:13).

Yet even in that glorious day of accomplishment, celebration, and dedication, Solomon acknowledged the limitations of an earthly temple. "But will God indeed dwell on the earth?" he asked before all the people. "Behold, heaven and the highest heaven cannot contain You, how much less this house which I have built!" (1 Kings 8:27).

The temple, a divinely inspired structure that God honored with his presence, could not hold all that he was. Given his people's habitual sin, even by the priests, the glory of God eventually left this magnificent building. By the time of Jeremiah, the Lord was calling into question the religious ceremonies of his chosen people: "Has this house, which is called by My name, become a den of robbers in your sight?" (Jer. 7:11).

Around the time Jeremiah was saying that, Josiah, a king "who turned to the LORD with all his heart and with all his soul and with all his might," cleaned up the temple, eliminating spiritists, mediums, idols, and other abominations. Even so, God was angry with the nation of Judah. He said, "I will remove Judah also from My sight, as I have removed Israel. And I will cast off Jerusalem, this city which I have chosen, and the temple of which I said, 'My name shall be there'" (2 Kings 23:24–27).

God abandoned his temple, and it was destroyed, as the prophets foretold, by the Babylonians in approximately 586 BC:

> The LORD, the God of their fathers, sent word to them again and again by His messengers, because He had compassion on His people and on His dwelling place; but they continually mocked the messengers of God, despised His words and scoffed at His prophets, until the wrath of the LORD arose against His people, until there was no remedy. Therefore He brought up against them the king of the Chaldeans who slew their young men with the sword in the house of their sanctuary, and had no compassion on young man or virgin, old man or infirm; He gave them all into his hand. All the articles of the house of God, great and small, and the treasures of the house of the LORD, and the treasures of the king and of his officers, he brought them all to Babylon. Then they burned the house of God and broke down the wall of Jerusalem, and burned all its fortified buildings with fire and destroyed all its valuable articles. (2 Chron. 36:15–19)

The remnant of survivors spent seventy years in captivity. It was only after that prophesied time was up that the Israelites were allowed to return to Jerusalem, where they rebuilt the temple under the governorship of Zerubbabel.

And so it was that God lived among his creation for a time in a tabernacle and then a temple, both built of strict obedience and mediated by men of ritual service, consecrated and atoned by blood sacrifice. Such an arrangement seems bizarre. But when understood in the context of the life, death, and resurrection of Jesus Christ, it begins to make sense.

Jesus and the Temple

Shortly after first manifesting his miraculous power at the wedding in Cana, Jesus went to Jerusalem to celebrate one of the most important rituals of Jewish faith: the Passover. But when he went to God's holy temple, he did not find the dwelling place of God. He did not step into an atmosphere of reverent worship, as one would expect when entering into a time of communion with the Most High God. Instead he found people selling cattle, sheep, and doves for a religious ritual of sacrifice. The original decree to make one's best sacrifice in an obedient act of faith was fulfilled by simply buying an animal at the temple to meet an inconvenient requirement.

The priests and the people were all complicit in their conspiracy that turned the personal act of true sacrifice into a down-and-dirty business transaction. Jesus fashioned a whip to drive the animals out of the temple courts, saying, "Take these things away; stop making My Father's house a place of business" (John 2:16). The idea of a holy sacrifice being turned into impersonal commerce offended Jesus. "It is written," he said, quoting Jeremiah, "'My house shall be called a house of prayer'; but you are making it a robbers' den" (Matt. 21:13).

The Jewish religious leaders, recognizing Jesus' references to the prophets and hearing his proclamation of God as his father, immediately questioned his authority. They demanded a miracle from him to prove his right to interfere (John 2:18). Jesus answered them in a way they did not understand, as was often the case with religious people he encountered. "'Destroy this temple, and in three days I will raise it up.' The Jews then said, 'It took forty-six years to build this temple, and will You raise it up in three days?'" (John 2:19–20). Jesus was revealing a truth that they could not grasp. Ever since the time of Moses, God had dwelled in a physical structure. Only special, select followers could enter into God's presence in the tabernacle or temple, and the requirements for such entry were rigorous and meticulous. But Jesus came to fulfill the old covenant. In doing so, he was the walking, breathing, speaking point of contact for man to meet God. The temple age was about to come to a close. The sacrifice of the Lamb of God was about to end the necessity for the blood of lambs to be shed on an altar of wood and stone. The apostle John understood what Jesus meant: "He was speaking of the temple of His body" (John 2:21).

Religion had made the temple into an idol. The lifeblood of the relationship between God and man—the sacrifice of pure animals—had become an abomination. The presence of holy God departed the dwelling place as Jesus died, yet the people continued observing empty traditions until the Romans razed it in AD 70.

By revealing this new and transforming truth about the temple—man's way to connect with God—being embodied in himself, Jesus tore down the notion that a building contained the presence of God. There was no longer a need for a structural temple of stone; it was now one of flesh and blood. What was once the way into God's presence was being replaced by the one who declared himself the Way.

So the first dwelling place of God in the New Testament was not the temple in Jerusalem; it was in the person of Jesus Christ. Then later, after Jesus ascended into heaven, Paul wrote to believers and said, "Do you not know that you are a temple of God and that the Spirit of God dwells in you? If any man destroys the temple of God, God will destroy him, for the temple of God is holy, and that is what you are" (1 Cor. 3:16–17). Paul affirmed that the point of connection with God shifted so that believers themselves became the dwelling place of God. We no longer have to go to a specific place to meet with him because the Holy Spirit dwells within us.

And just in case anyone was tempted to continue looking to Jerusalem for his presence, Jesus laid that to rest when he foretold the destruction of the second temple. He said, "Not one stone here will be left upon another, which will not be torn down" (Matt. 24:2).

This of course piqued the disciples' curiosity, and they pressed him on it. Jesus then launched into a lengthy prophecy, telling the disciples that they would be persecuted and killed (which they were) and that war would come (which it did). He told them to flee to the hills of Judea when they saw what the prophet Daniel called "the abomination of desolation" standing in the temple (Matt. 24:15).

But unlike Daniel's prophetic vision of the destruction of the second temple, Jesus' prophecy was not for a time in the distant future. It was, in Jesus' words, "near." In fact, it was "right at the door" (Matt. 24:33).

"This generation will not pass away until all these things take place," Jesus told them (Matt. 24:34). In saying this, Jesus was not only preparing his followers for the tribulation that was to come over the next few decades, but he was also anchoring them in faith for those most difficult of times. John the Baptist and the apostle James were both beheaded. Tradition holds that Philip preached in Phrygia (modern-day Turkey) and was martyred there. Bartholomew spread the gospel to Armenia and India and reportedly was skinned alive and then beheaded. Thomas is said to have traveled to southern India, where he was eventually speared to death. Other disciples met equally horrifying ends. Only John is believed to have died an old man, but even he suffered great persecution.

Through it all their faith never wavered. Every prophecy and promise came true, fueling their belief in Jesus' words and works. When the time came for the destruction of the second temple in Jerusalem, those who knew Jesus were not caught off guard.

The Veil

Before this final destruction came to pass, though, just after Jesus died on the cross, something happened at the temple to signal the shift that was coming. Although the temple provided a place for man to be close to God's presence, an important part of the temple separated them. This was the temple veil. It was four inches thick and woven of blue, purple, and scarlet linen, as commanded. It bore the images of cherubim and shielded the Holy of Holies from the Holy Place. The room where the ark of the covenant and its mercy seat resided and where God appeared remained apart from the place where the high priest entered. Only once a year, on the Day of Atonement, could the high priest actually pass through the veil to enter the Holy of Holies, and then only after donning designated attire, washing according to ritual, and using the smoke of incense to cloud his vision. The temple veil not only served as the divider between God and man, but it was protection for the high priest. Any unauthorized entry resulted in immediate death.

God warned Moses at the outset of the construction of the tabernacle, saying, "Tell your brother Aaron that he shall not enter at any time into the holy place inside the veil, before the mercy seat which is on the ark, or he will die; for I will appear in the cloud over the mercy seat" (Lev. 16:2). The veil was such a holy necessity that, when dissembling and reassembling the tabernacle, only certain priests were allowed to handle it. To Aaron, God said, "You and your sons with you shall attend to your priesthood for everything concerning the altar and inside the veil, and you are to perform service. I am giving you the priesthood as a bestowed service, but the outsider who comes near shall be put to death" (Num. 18:7).

The veil was serious business.

The prophet Isaiah looked forward to the day when the veil would be removed. He said that when that time came, "The LORD of hosts will prepare a lavish banquet for all peoples on this mountain; / A banquet of aged wine, choice pieces with marrow, / And refined, aged wine." The imagery of a feast would have resonated with the Israelites. The coming celebration would bring nourishment for the soul and atonement for sin. He continued, "And on this mountain [Zion in Jerusalem] He will swallow up the covering which is over all peoples, / Even the veil which is stretched over all nations." God gave the law to Moses on a mountain, and he would symbolically return to a mountain to remove the veil separating God and man. Furthermore,

> He will swallow up death for all time,
> And the Lord GOD will wipe tears away from all faces,
> And He will remove the reproach of His people from all the earth;
> For the LORD has spoken.
> And it will be said in that day,
> "Behold, this is our God for whom we have waited that He might
> save us.
> This is the LORD for whom we have waited;
> Let us rejoice and be glad in His salvation." (Isa. 25:6–9)

Isaiah's glimpse into the nature of the Messiah's work foretold many things, among them the removal of the veil. Though it was primarily symbolic in nature, there would be a physical manifestation as God tore down this division.

As Jesus was crucified, an amazing and terrifying thing happened. At the moment he "cried out again with a loud voice, and yielded up His spirit," the gospel of Matthew tells us, "the veil of the temple was torn in two from top to bottom" (27:50–51). Any priest who was present or found it torn shortly thereafter must have been in fear for his life. But the reality was that this event initiated new life.

That veil was sixty feet high and four inches thick. And notice it was torn from top to bottom. Ripping it was no small feat. The next verse in this gospel account tells of an earthquake, so it is possible that the quake caused the tear, but it's pretty obvious who caused the quake! When Jesus died, he brought down the barrier between man and God. When he rose again, he stole death's power. And when he sent the Holy Spirit, the Holy of Holies could no longer contain the divine presence on the earth. Instead of fearing God's presence, we can now take refuge in it. This hope is set in front of us, the writer of Hebrews said, "as an anchor of the soul, a hope both sure and steadfast and one which enters within the veil" (6:19).

For those who believe in Jesus Christ, there is no more veil, for "whenever a person turns to the Lord, the veil is taken away" (2 Cor. 3:16). We enter the holy place by the blood of Jesus. He allows us to stand fearlessly in his presence.

A Living Temple

When Jesus walked the earth, the issue of the temple came up in the most unlikely of places—in Samaria as he was traveling from Judea to Galilee. Given the tension between the mixed-race Samaritans, who held to the law as best they could, and the Jews, who claimed a blood right to the law, many Jews circumvented Samaria on their journeys, preferring to go around rather than through this land of "mongrels." But Jesus went right through it, stopping along the way at an old watering hole called "Jacob's well."

There he encountered a Samaritan woman. He asked her for a

drink, which surprised her because Jews typically did not even speak to Samaritans. "How is it that You, being a Jew, ask me for a drink since I am a Samaritan woman?" she asked (John 4:9). Jesus began to talk to her about the spring of eternal life, referring to himself. He told her about her past and present, prompting her to observe that he was a prophet.

Her next question revealed Samaritan-Jewish controversy regarding the temple. Given all of the things she could have asked him, she chose to ask about the true location of worship, where the faithful should go to meet with God.

When Moses and the Israelites crossed the Jordan River, they were commanded to build an altar. Blessings and curses were proclaimed, with the blessings being bestowed from Mount Gerizim (Deut. 27:12). It was here that the Samaritans later erected a temple, possibly around the time of Nehemiah. This became a sticking point between Samaritans and Jews. In fact, Jews would only accept Samaritans into Judaism when they rejected their belief in Mount Gerizim.

When the Greek king Antiochus IV Epiphanes rose up against the Jews in both Judea and Samaria, fighting against the rebellious Maccabees, he converted the temple at Gerizim into a shrine for Zeus. The Maccabeean leader and Jewish high priest Yohanan Hyrcanus destroyed that temple around 110 BC, but this didn't eliminate the Samaritans' practice of gathering at Mount Gerizim. They still assembled at the mountain to worship.

So the woman, perceiving Jesus as a man of spiritual insight, brought up the issue that proved religious authenticity in their time. "Our fathers worshiped in this mountain, and you people say that in Jerusalem is the place where men ought to worship" (John 4:20). I find this exchange rather humorous. The woman at the well typifies religious humanity. She was sitting there with the God of the universe, the promised Messiah, the Savior of all mankind, and she basically asked, "Who's right, them or us?" I imagine Jesus answered her with a bit of a smile. He was offering her the eternal light of the world, and she wanted to discuss the shadows.

He graciously dropped an atomic bomb of truth on her.

"Woman, believe Me, an hour is coming when neither in this mountain nor in Jerusalem will you worship the Father. You worship what you do not know; we worship what we know, for salvation is from the Jews. But an hour is coming, and now is, when the true worshipers will worship the Father in spirit and truth; for such people the Father seeks to be His worshipers. God is spirit, and those who worship Him must worship in spirit and truth." (John 4:21–24)

Jesus elevated the discussion beyond the idea of a physical temple. Note the time frame of the change in worship that he mentioned: it was both coming and already there. The temple was still significant, but the arrival of Christ was more significant. The old existed, but the new had arrived. The old would soon pass away, and the new would operate exclusively from then on. Worship would no longer be bound to a building. It would explode wherever his spirit and truth carried it. Her interest in the true temple was relegated to the past even as she encountered the living temple in the present. The relevancy of Christ made the temple irrelevant.

After Christ's death, resurrection, and ascension, the disciples began preaching the gospel to the Jewish nations and beyond. When Paul went to Athens to preach to the Greeks, he stood on Mars Hill and said,

"The God who made the world and all things in it, since He is Lord of heaven and earth, does not dwell in temples made with hands; nor is He served by human hands, as though He needed anything, since He Himself gives to all people life and breath and all things; and He made from one man every nation of mankind to live on all the face of the earth." (Acts 17:24–26)

The gospel that began with the Jews quickly encompassed "every nation of mankind" and the temple no longer contained the Spirit of God, even though the second temple of Zerubbabel still stood in Jerusalem at the time.

When Paul wrote to the various first-century churches in what would become our New Testament, he completely redefined the concept of the temple. It was a radical departure from the historical context, echoing Christ and spiritualizing what had been a physical pillar of the Jewish faith. He harkened back to the words of Isaiah to make his case.

> For we are the temple of the living God; just as God said,
>> "I will dwell in them and walk among them;
>> And I will be their God, and they shall be My people.
>> Therefore, come out from their midst and be separate," says the
>>> Lord.
>> "And do not touch what is unclean;
>> And I will welcome you.
>> And I will be a father to you,
>> And you shall be sons and daughters to Me,"
>> Says the Lord Almighty. (2 Cor. 6:16–18)

This is the essence of the temple truth. In the Old Testament, God's Spirit inhabited the temple until the Israelites' sin drove him away. Since the New Testament, God's Spirit inhabits people—those who believe in Jesus Christ. He dwells with us and walks with us, not in any structure created by us.

Peter picked up on this theme as well. He called both Jewish and non-Jewish believers "living stones" who were "being built up as a spiritual house" (1 Peter 2:5). This is the great promise of the temple. The picture of a place where God resides, manifesting his power, has become a reality within the lives of everyone who believes in Christ, who is the cornerstone of this new, living temple. The attention to detail, the significance of being set apart, and the honor of his abiding presence all comes together in you!

The End of the Temple

In the year AD 70 (about thirty-seven years after Jesus' crucifixion and resurrection), the Roman general Titus surrounded Jerusalem for the final assault. The historian Josephus recorded many of the horrors of this first-century holocaust as the Romans mercilessly attacked Jerusalem during the Passover: "Neither did any other city ever suffer such miseries, nor did any age ever breed a generation more fruitful in wickedness than this was."[2]

Thousands of Jews died of starvation, while others descended into madness that included cannibalism. By the historian's account, "the upper rooms were full of women and children that were dying by famine."[3] The Romans penetrated the walls of the city, and "they caught every day five hundred Jews; nay, some days they caught more" and crucified them. "Out of the wrath and hatred they bore the Jews, nailed those they caught, one after one way, and another after another, to the crosses, by way of jest, when their multitude was so great, that room was wanting for the crosses, and crosses wanting for the bodies."[4]

Many deserted the city in hopes of surviving among the Romans. At one point, it was rumored that the Jews had swallowed their gold in order to retrieve it later from their own excrement. When the Romans heard this, they slaughtered the deserters and dissected them to search for gold. "In one night's time about two thousand of these deserters were thus dissected," Josephus wrote.[5]

By the time the city and the temple were destroyed, an estimated 1.1 million people had perished and another ninety-seven thousand were taken captive. Not only was the temple burned to the ground, but the soldiers had sifted through the fiery remains for valuables, including the traces of gold within the walls. Indeed, every stone was thrown down.

The followers of Jesus who fled when the Romans desecrated the religious place understood once again that Jesus' words were true. The earthly temple fell, but the earthly embodiment of God now stood "at the right hand of the Father," a place of honor and authority (Luke 22:69).

Jesus replaced the temple and its rituals and sacrifices. The old covenant was fulfilled, and the shadows of its ways disappeared as the Light of the World shone in full glory. The old age ended, and a new day had fully arrived.

Jews who reject the divinity of Christ understandably still seek the restoration of the temple in Jerusalem. If Jesus Christ were not the promised Messiah, this makes complete sense. Currently, they have a political problem with Muslims occupying the Temple Mount. They also have religious problems of ritual purification, altar location, and high priest appointment.

But if Jesus Christ is the Messiah, as Christians believe, then reconstructing a temple is not only a waste of time but a step backward. If we live in a time when we do not worship in Gerizim, Jerusalem, or any other so-called holy site, then all of our efforts should seek to build up the spiritual temple, which is in the people we call the church. God doesn't want a building; he wants "living stones." The past looks to a structure, but the future looks to a society.

The message of Christ is that God does not dwell in a single physical location, regardless of its history or sentimental value. He lives in his people. Whenever and wherever we come together under his authority and direction, the cloud of his glory appears.

Living the Promise

Understanding this New Testament dynamic should do several things in the life of a believer. First, we should recognize the massive blessing he has given to us. Whereas the Old Testament priests had to follow strict regulations regarding the temple in order to receive God's presence, our transposed reality should cause us to respond with as much attention to detail. Because his Spirit resides in us, we should seek purity in our thoughts and actions. When believers are quick or casual about profaning his temple, so to speak, it reflects an ignorance or unawareness of the glory he has given to us. We take it too lightly, too easily. We are his temple, his place of residency, the place where the Most High meets us on a deep and personal level. Once that truth settles in, the thought of turning his temple into a whorehouse of worldly lovers becomes repugnant and intolerable.

Next, we should take advantage of the portable nature of his temple. We don't have to go to church to commune with God. Nor do we have to get others to enter a building in order for them to experience his presence. We *should* gather with other believers, and we *should* invite others in, but we *should not* limit our encounters with

God to a location. We can and should encounter him daily in the temple that Christ established, which is us.

By inviting others into our lives, we invite them into his temple as well, where they can encounter his glory and presence. That means you can worship anywhere—your home, office, school, the back of a cab—wherever! And you can present God to others whenever and wherever—in a park, over lunch, on an airplane, in a prison—it doesn't matter. Sins can be forgiven, atonement made, and lives eternally changed, all by entering into God's presence by way of a "temple" that is you.

Finally, we can quit looking for God to restore a physical temple to fulfill his will on earth. He has already established his earthly residence in temples of flesh and blood. Too many people are looking to restore an obsolete building. This just leads to a lot of waiting when we should be moving. The age of the physical temple is in the past. The new-covenant journey is under way, so it's time to join it. It was already at Jacob's well, so expecting some physical, outward expression of a spiritual, inner truth is to miss it. Jesus Christ established his temple on earth, and it's you. The debate is settled, so the time for arguing is past. It's time for living it.

CHAPTER 7

The Promise of Judgment

"He who believes in Him is not judged; he who
does not believe has been judged already."
JOHN 3:18

I was raised to think I would one day stand in heaven with God, the angels, and every believer who ever lived while my whole life was projected on a giant movie screen for all to see. Every mistake would be viewed in full color with surround sound. Even my thoughts would be heard, as a voiceover narrating the worst of me. Jesus' words were quoted with full King James authority: "For nothing is secret, that shall not be made manifest; neither any thing hid, that shall not be known and come abroad" (Luke 8:17 KJV). Obviously, Jesus was talking about big movie screens in that parable!

Of course, this expectation didn't square with passages talking about God's grace covering our sin or his forgiveness removing them as far as the east is from the west. But when you've got a narrative going, why ruin it with the totality of Scripture? Sarcasm aside, the idea that payment will someday be due for all our wrongdoing persists in many circles.

That's why perhaps the most unexpected promise emerging from the shadows of the old covenant is that of judgment. The word alone conjures images of wrath, destruction, condemnation, and fear. We see the judgment of God as punishment for every mistake we've ever made, whether intentional or unintentional, known or unknown, big or small. The prophets of old issued long and detailed predictions of terrifying judgment, and we tend to transfer these to the new covenant. Question most people in a church, and they will admit that the idea of judgment makes them uncomfortable, overwhelmed, or frightened. We don't like to think about it because we all know, deep down inside, that we deserve to be judged harshly and mercilessly.

Fortunately, that is not the fate of Christians. When taken in context of the whole Bible, the Old Testament view of God's judgment makes sense, but the New Testament result of Christ's judgment holds something we should not dread. In fact *judgment*, which simply means "the act of deciding a case," gives us cause for hope, celebration, and immense gratitude. When we understand what judgment is, how it has been enacted, and what it holds for the future, then we see the wonderful promise for each of us.

Warnings

The prophets in the Old Testament were pretty terrifying. When it came to the topic of judgment, they always seemed to predict untold horrors. Hosea said, "Therefore I have hewn them in pieces by the prophets; / I have slain them by the words of My mouth; / And the judgments on you are like the light that goes forth" (Hos. 6:5). Isaiah said, "Behold, the LORD lays the earth waste, devastates it, distorts its surface and scatters its inhabitants" (Isa. 24:1). Jeremiah said, "Therefore, thus says the LORD, the God of hosts, / 'Because you have spoken this word, / Behold, I am making My words in your mouth fire / And this people wood, and it will consume them'" (Jer. 5:14). Ezekiel quoted God as saying, "So it will be a reproach, a reviling, a warning and an object of horror to the nations who surround you when I execute judgments against you in anger, wrath and raging rebukes. I, the LORD, have spoken" (Ezek. 5:15).

We know the stories of Noah, the destruction of Sodom and Gomorrah, the plagues in Egypt, and other frightening tales. No wonder when we think of judgment, we think in terms of flood, fire, war, and death. This is how God balanced the scales of justice for centuries. Wickedness birthed destruction.

Near the end of the Southern Kingdom of Judah, two hundred years after the Northern Kingdom of Israel had fallen, the prophet Zephaniah penned his warning of judgment during the reign of Josiah. The priesthood was corrupt, the people wicked, and the end near. Within a generation, the Babylonians would conquer Jerusalem, ending the Israelite nation and sending the people into exile.

As was typical of the old prophets, Zephaniah wrote in the first person, in God's voice. He began by dealing with the Jews: "I will stretch out My hand against Judah / And against all the inhabitants of Jerusalem" (Zeph. 1:4). He told of utter destruction. In the hyperbolic language of prophecy, he said God would remove all living things from the face of the earth. He spoke of "the day of the LORD," which would be "a day of wrath . . . / A day of trouble and distress, / A day of destruction and desolation, / A day of darkness and gloom, / A day of clouds and thick darkness" (Zeph. 1:14–15).

Next, he dealt with the pagan nations around Judah: "Surely Moab will be like Sodom / And the sons of Ammon like Gomorrah— / A place possessed by nettles and salt pits, / And a perpetual desolation" (Zeph. 2:9). Zephaniah said God would destroy Assyria, Gaza, Ashod, Canaan, and others. He also called out the city of Nineveh, which had been spared previously because they repented when Jonah was sent. However, the city and entire Assyrian region had grown wicked once again, and Zephaniah promised that "the LORD [would] be terrifying to them" (Zeph. 2:11). For all of this, he set a timeline: "near and coming very quickly" (Zeph. 1:14).

Zephaniah then circled back to Jerusalem, calling it "the tyrannical city." He condemned God's chosen people, saying, "Her prophets are reckless, treacherous men; / Her priests have profaned the sanctuary. / They have done violence to the law" (Zeph. 3:1, 4). God promised to pour out his "indignation" and "burning anger" so that "all the earth will be devoured / By the fire of My zeal" (Zeph. 3:8). (Note the use of "all the earth." This is a metaphor describing all the parts of the world known to the author and readers, as we will see.)

Then Zephaniah did what prophets typically did. He told of a restoration. "Then I will give to the peoples purified lips, / That all of them may call on the name of the LORD, / To serve Him shoulder to shoulder" (Zeph. 3:9). Notice that he said "peoples." During an age when only the Israelites' descendants were God's chosen people, Zephaniah foretold a time when all who called on the name of the Lord would serve him together as one. He ended by reasserting, "Indeed, I will give you renown and praise / Among *all the peoples of the earth*, / When I restore your fortunes before your eyes" (Zeph. 3:20, emphasis added).

Regarding subsequent judgment, he said, "The LORD has taken

away His judgments against you, / He has cleared away your enemies. / The King of Israel, the LORD, is in your midst; / You will fear disaster no more" (Zeph. 3:15).

Some theologians date Zephaniah's writing around 640 BC. Nineveh was destroyed in 612 BC, and Judah fell in 586 BC. A generation later, the people began returning from Babylonian exile and reconstructing the temple that so many prophets had foretold. Israel became a nation again, though ruled by other empires most of the time (the Maccabean rule excepted). God would give them another chance, but they would fail. It would still be some time before the final King of Israel, Jesus, was in their midst, would gather all the peoples of the earth to him, and would take away all of God's judgments so that people would never again fear divine disaster.

But first, justice was due. The great and terrible day of the Lord was still on the horizon.

The Last Prophet

An estimated two hundred years after Zephaniah's prophecy, Zerubbabel's temple had been built, and Jews had reestablished themselves in Jerusalem and throughout Judea. However, the priesthood was again corrupt and the people wicked. The priests were presenting lame and sick animals for sacrifice in direct defiance of the law. They were robbing God by withholding the tithes. They were declaring evil to be good and acceptable by God. In response, the Lord didn't just threaten to withhold their blessings; he said he would curse their blessings. It doesn't get much worse than that, but to illustrate the point, he said, "I will spread refuse on your faces" (Mal. 2:3). The prophet Malachi again delivered the dual messages of judgment and restoration.

Malachi foretold the coming of John the Baptist, whom he called the Lord's messenger, who would "clear the way before Me" (Mal. 3:1). He referred to him as "Elijah the prophet before the coming of the great and terrible day of the LORD" (Mal. 4:5). He also spoke of Jesus Christ, saying, "The messenger of the covenant, in whom you delight, behold, He is coming" (Mal. 3:1). He said God would "suddenly come to His temple" (Mal. 3:1), and the judgment he would bring would consume everything known to the Jewish people. The very foundations would be shaken. "The day is coming, burning like a furnace; and all the arrogant and every evildoer will be chaff; and the day that is coming will set them ablaze, . . . so that it will leave them neither root nor branch" (Mal. 4:1).

Yet in the middle of this frightening reckoning of all their wrongs, God extended an invitation to reconcile with him. "Return to Me, and I will return to you," he promised (Mal. 3:7).

Judgment was due. It was coming. But an escape plan had been prepared. God repeatedly demonstrated that he was both patient and just. He would not overlook evil, but he would always make a gracious offer to restore those who would stop doing evil and return to him. His judgment was harsh because it was just, but his kindness was unparalleled because he offered forgiveness. He warned his people over and over until he came to meet with them face-to-face. Then he would warn them in person, all while extending mercy and grace to those who would receive it.

Jesus and Judgment

Before John the Baptist was born, the angel Gabriel came to his father, a priest named Zacharias, and told him his wife, Elizabeth, would bear a son. The angel quoted Malachi in laying out the child's destiny: "It is he who will go as a forerunner before Him in the spirit and power of Elijah, *to turn the hearts of the fathers back to the children*, and the disobedient to the attitude of the righteous, so as to make ready a people prepared for the Lord" (Luke 1:17, emphasis added).

This child, known as John the Baptist, was also prophesied by Isaiah:

> A voice is calling,
> "Clear the way for the LORD in the wilderness;
> Make smooth in the desert a highway for our God.
> Let every valley be lifted up,
> And every mountain and hill be made low;
> And let the rough ground become a plain,
> And the rugged terrain a broad valley;
> Then the glory of the LORD will be revealed,
> And all flesh will see it together;
> For the mouth of the LORD has spoken." (Isa. 40:3–5)

Note the prophetic language used by Isaiah. Valleys would rise, mountains would crumble, and the rugged terrain would become flat. John the Baptist didn't literally carve out highways in the mountains. He spiritually carved out the path for Jesus Christ as he preached the arrival of the Messiah. He also spoke of the coming judgment. "You brood of vipers," he said to the Jewish crowds,

> "who warned you to flee from the wrath to come? Therefore bear fruits in keeping with repentance, and do not begin to say to yourselves, 'We have Abraham for our father,' for I say to you that from these stones God is able to raise up children to Abraham. Indeed the

axe is already laid at the root of the trees; so every tree that does not bear good fruit is cut down and thrown into the fire." (Luke 3:7–9)

Jesus was that ax. Unlike the pruning of branches, which trims the dead parts from the tree to improve its health, a full-fledged chopping down was about to take place. The picture is of a woodsman who has decided which tree to cut down and lays his ax at the root of the tree while he takes off his jacket or further prepares for the work. God had decided the days of pruning his chosen people were over. He would bring the whole tree down through the work of Jesus Christ. And it would happen soon.

Just before his crucifixion, as he dined and shared in what's called the Lord's Supper with his disciples, Jesus used the same analogy of the tree to explain his relationship to his followers and the fate of those who rejected him.

> "I am the true vine, and My Father is the vinedresser. Every branch in Me that does not bear fruit, He takes away; and every branch that bears fruit, He prunes it so that it may bear more fruit. You are already clean because of the word which I have spoken to you. Abide in Me, and I in you. As the branch cannot bear fruit of itself unless it abides in the vine, so neither can you unless you abide in Me. I am the vine, you are the branches; he who abides in Me and I in him, he bears much fruit, for apart from Me you can do nothing. If anyone does not abide in Me, he is thrown away as a branch and dries up; and they gather them, and cast them into the fire and they are burned." (John 15:1–6)

Again we see the idea of cutting off the dead parts and throwing them into the fire. This is the image of judgment.

But note what Jesus said to his disciples: "You are already clean." The Greek word translated "clean" is *katharos*, from which we derive *catharsis*. It means clear, pure, and free from guilt. It's the same word Jesus used when he spoke of Judas Iscariot, saying, "Not all of you are clean" (John 13:11). It's also the same word he spoke in the Sermon on the Mount, saying, "Blessed are the pure in heart" (Matt. 5:8). Jesus explained how they had been purified and pruned, saying it was through God's word which he had spoken and they had received. This was the process by which they would escape the coming judgment.

It's easy for us to view judgment through human eyes, but that misses the purpose and method of God. The disciples—those purified through his word and exempt from being cast into the fire—suffered tremendously. Some were beaten, tortured, imprisoned, and killed. John the Baptist was beheaded. It would be tempting to call that some form of God's judgment, but it wasn't. It would also be easy to think that escaping judgment means escaping pain or death. Again, that's wrong. Persecution is not judgment. Judgment is the deciding of a case and the execution of a sentence.[1]

Believers who suffer for the cause of Christ are, in a sense, judged, but the judgment is all good. "Blessed are those who have been persecuted for the sake of righteousness, for theirs is the kingdom of heaven," Jesus said (Matt. 5:10). That's how he decides that case. But the judgment to destruction is entirely different. The cutting off and casting into the fire would happen soon. The day of judgment was coming quickly, because the woodsman had decided it was time to bring down an entire economy. Jesus Christ came, delivered God's word, and turned many children's hearts back to the Father. But for those who refused, only producing bad fruit, the time for pruning was over. This time, the ax would fall.

The Day of the Lord

John the Baptist also said of the coming Christ, "His winnowing fork is in His hand to thoroughly clear His threshing floor, and to gather the wheat into His barn; but He will burn up the chaff with unquenchable fire" (Luke 3:17).

After Jesus Christ rode into Jerusalem on a donkey at the beginning of the Passover Feast, he told a group of people, "Now judgment is upon this world" (John 12:31). The time had come for God to decide the case of the Israelites, and he handed that deliberation over to his Son.

After Jesus healed a man who had been born blind, the Jewish leaders cross-examined him. They had threatened to excommunicate from the synagogue anyone who called Jesus the Messiah, a serious punishment for Jews. Now they pressed this formerly blind man about Jesus, demanding that he give glory to God and not to Christ, whom they called a sinner.

"Whether He is a sinner, I do not know," the man said, "one thing I do know, that though I was blind, now I see." The man refused to denounce Christ and rebuked the Jewish leaders, so they kicked him out.

Jesus heard that they had put him out, and finding him, He said, "Do you believe in the Son of Man?" He answered, "Who is He, Lord, that I may believe in Him?" Jesus said to him, "You have both seen Him, and He is the one who is talking with you." And he said, "Lord, I believe." And he worshiped Him. And Jesus said, "For judgment I came into this world, so that those who do not see may see, and that those who see may become blind." Those of the Pharisees who were with Him heard these things and said to Him, "We are not blind too, are we?" Jesus said to them, "If you were blind, you would have no sin; but since you say, 'We see,' your sin remains." (John 9:24–25, 35–41)

This is a great picture of judgment. If we admit our blindness and believe in Christ, he opens our eyes and calls us clean. If we think we can see on our own, he leaves us in our sin, which leads to destruction. On this day, he passed judgment on those Jewish leaders, but not to destruction. For them, there was still time. The winnowing fork was in his hand and, like a farmer separating the wheat from the waste, he was separating belief from unbelief.

Jesus did this repeatedly on an individual basis throughout his ministry. After his death and resurrection, he sent his disciples to "all the nations" to preach one last time before wielding the winnowing fork over the whole nation, gathering the wheat for himself. Then when the winnowing was done, he would burn the chaff with unquenchable fire.

The day of the Lord was always prophesied to come with a combination of destruction and redemption. When Isaiah foresaw the judgment of Babylon, he said, "Wail, for the day of the LORD is near! / It will come as destruction from the Almighty. / Therefore all hands will fall limp, / And every man's heart will melt. . . . Behold, the day of the LORD is coming, / Cruel, with fury and burning anger, / To make the land a desolation" (Isa. 13:6–7, 9).

Ezekiel declared similar destruction on Egypt (Ezek. 30). Obadiah, Ezekiel, and Jeremiah all spoke of the fate of Edom, a powerful enemy of Israel whose capital, Petra, was one of the most magnificent cities in the world. (It was made famous to my generation in the movie *Indiana Jones and the Last Crusade*.) "For the day of the LORD draws near on all the nations," Obadiah wrote. "As you have done, it will be done to you. / Your dealings will return on your own head" (Obad. 1:15). About a hundred years after Obadiah's final warning, the Edomites were conquered.

To the wayward Israelites, Amos offered God's rebuke: "Alas, you who are longing for the day of the LORD, / For what purpose will the day of the LORD be to you? / It will be darkness and not light" (Amos 5:18). Within their generation, the Northern Kingdom of Israel fell to the Assyrians.

A century later, Zephaniah offered the same warning to Judah:

> Near is the great day of the LORD,
> Near and coming very quickly;
> Listen, the day of the LORD!
> In it the warrior cries out bitterly.
> A day of wrath is that day,
> A day of trouble and distress,
> A day of destruction and desolation,
> A day of darkness and gloom,
> A day of clouds and thick darkness,
> A day of trumpet and battle cry
> Against the fortified cities
> And the high corner towers.
> I will bring distress on men
> So that they will walk like the blind,
> Because they have sinned against the LORD. (Zeph. 1:14–17)

Within their generation, Judah fell to the Babylonians.

Before either kingdom had fallen, and about eight hundred years before Jesus' resurrection, the prophet Joel foresaw the day of the Lord in relation to Christ. He spoke of judgment on the Israelites, employing the usual apocalyptic language of "darkness and gloom" and "clouds and thick darkness" (Joel 2:2). He then promised redemption in a season, saying, "The threshing floors will be full of grain, / And the vats will overflow with the new wine and oil" (Joel 2:24). Interestingly, he further made the prediction that Peter would later claim to be fulfilled at Pentecost:

> "It will come about after this
> That I will pour out My Spirit on all mankind;
> And your sons and daughters will prophesy,
> Your old men will dream dreams,
> Your young men will see visions.
> Even on the male and female servants
> I will pour out My Spirit in those days.
> I will display wonders in the sky and on the earth,
> Blood, fire and columns of smoke.
> The sun will be turned into darkness
> And the moon into blood
> Before the great and awesome day of the LORD comes.
> And it will come about that whoever calls on the name of the LORD
> Will be delivered;
> For on Mount Zion and in Jerusalem
> There will be those who escape,
> As the LORD has said,
> Even among the survivors whom the LORD calls. (Joel 2:28–32)

This is perhaps the clearest explanation of what prophetic language looks like in the natural. At Pentecost, the Holy Spirit filled the Jewish believers gathered in a house, and they began proclaiming the gospel in multiple languages. They were the native dialects of the Jews in Jerusalem who had returned from all across the Middle East,

Europe, Asia, and Africa. The book of Acts even includes the visual elements of the ancient prophecy—blood, fire, smoke, darkness— though it was probably not literal. The prophetic language reflected the spiritual ramifications as Peter preached his sermon, and the "new wine and oil" poured out. It was the spark that ignited Christianity and sent it on a global trajectory.

But, according to Joel, there was destruction to follow, "for the day of the LORD is near in the valley of decision" (Joel 3:14). The nations surrounding Israel that had abused God's people for so long would face destruction as God brought his judgment, deciding the case for those who rejected his Son and blessing those forever who embraced him.

What would this judgment look like? We know that when Jesus walked, winnowing fork in hand as he sifted the wheat of believers from the chaff of unbelievers, there was no great physical destruction. Throughout the epistles there is no record of it either. But both Christ and the various writers of the rest of our New Testament spoke of a coming judgment. One that was coming soon.

In Paul's first letter to the church in Thessalonica, he said, "For you yourselves know full well that the day of the Lord will come just like a thief in the night." This frightening fate was not for believers, however. "But you, brethren," Paul continued, "are not in darkness, that the day would overtake you like a thief" (1 Thess. 5:2, 4).

In his second letter to them, he said, "Now we request you, brethren, with regard to the coming of our Lord Jesus Christ and our gathering together to Him, that you not be quickly shaken from your composure or be disturbed either by a spirit or a message or a letter as if from us, to the effect that the day of the Lord has come" (2 Thess. 2:1–2). He was telling them that this day of the Lord had not yet come. He said it was "already at work" and would happen "in order that they all may be judged who did not believe the truth, but took pleasure in wickedness" (2 Thess. 2:7, 12). He urged the believers there to "stand firm and hold to the traditions which you were taught" (2 Thess. 2:15). Why? Because something big was about to happen. Something terrible for those who "did not believe the truth." The day of the Lord would come to fulfillment with destruction for those who rejected Christ and salvation for those who believed.

The Wrath of God

Judgment to destruction is the fate of all who do not believe in Christ, whether Jew or Gentile. Likewise, redemption is the destiny of all who believe, whether Jew or Gentile. This is tied directly to the law. Wrath is God's expression of judgment for the purpose of destruction. It is reserved for those without faith in Christ, because it is only in him we find right standing with God.

"For the promise to Abraham or to his descendants that he would be heir of the world was not through the Law, but through the righteousness of faith," Paul explained to the Roman church. "For if those who are of the Law are heirs, faith is made void and the promise is nullified; for the Law brings about wrath, but where there is no law, there also is no violation" (Rom. 4:13–15).

Wrath is brought by the law. This is why Christians need not fear the wrath (the judgment to destruction) of God. It was targeted specifically to those under the old covenant. The writer of Hebrews explored it in detail. After laying out the new covenant established through Christ and debunking the idea that the old law was still necessary (a teaching prevalent at the time), he warned, "For if we go on sinning willfully after receiving the knowledge of the truth, there no longer remains a sacrifice for sins, but a terrifying expectation of judgment and the fury of a fire which will consume the adversaries." Rejecting Christ left no sacrifice great enough to cover one's sin. Only destructive judgment remained. Those who continued in unbelief "insulted the Spirit of grace." He then reminded them of the words of the Torah—"Vengeance is Mine, I will repay"—and the psalmist— "The Lord will judge His people." He finished with the warning, "It is a terrifying thing to fall into the hands of the living God" (Heb. 10:26–31).

Rejecting Christ should be a terrifying prospect, but this fear should not plague the hearts of Christians who have been covered by Jesus' sacrifice. The problem is that many churches use Old Testament passages to instill fear in believers. Even good-hearted preachers who do not fully understand the new-covenant age in which we live perpetuate this fear-based motive for good conduct. Certainly the realization of judgment and eternal separation from God should open up nonbelievers to the gospel, but it's God's kindness that brings about repentance (Rom. 2:4). Yes, the wrath of God is real. It's written about throughout the Bible and displayed throughout history. But it is also absolutely, 100 percent bought and paid for by the blood of Christ.

"Walk by the Spirit, and you will not carry out the desire of the flesh," Paul wrote. "For the flesh sets its desire against the Spirit, and the Spirit against the flesh; for these are in opposition to one another, so that you may not do the things that you please. But if you are led by the Spirit, you are not under the Law" (Gal. 5:16–18). Who is led by the Spirit? All who are not under the law, meaning all who believe in Jesus Christ. We are not perfect, but we are being perfected. We war against our old natures, but with the guarantee of victory. Through him we are no longer slaves to sin. We will not taste death but have eternal life, and we do not and will not face condemnation:

Therefore there is now no condemnation for those who are in Christ Jesus. For the law of the Spirit of life in Christ Jesus has set you free from the law of sin and of death. For what the Law could not do, weak as it was through the flesh, God did: sending His own Son in the likeness of sinful flesh and as an offering for sin, He condemned sin in the flesh, so that the requirement of the Law might be fulfilled in us, who do not walk according to the flesh but according to the Spirit. (Rom. 8:1–4)

The law was fulfilled in Christ. When we are born of the Spirit, we are no longer under the law. We do not have a future of wrath but of forgiveness. This is the promise of judgment: we do not face destruction, only redemption.

Judgment for Christians

There is one judgment that we will face, in the sense of God deciding our case. When you understand that we are not subject to wrath, but only to grace, this is good news. "Blessed are those whose lawless deeds have been forgiven, / And whose sins have been covered," Paul wrote, quoting David. "Blessed is the man whose sin the Lord will not take into account" (Rom. 4:7–8). In Christ, sin is forgiven. Transgressions are removed. Iniquity is swallowed in salvation.

The writer of Hebrews called God "a consuming fire" (Heb. 12:29). When John the Baptist foretold Christ's works, he said, "He will baptize you with the Holy Spirit and fire" (Matt. 3:11). Fire is destructive, but it purifies. Fire destroys the junk. Paul explained this dynamic by first establishing the unshakable foundation on which we stand. Then he showed how we can build on that foundation:

According to the grace of God which was given to me, like a wise master builder I laid a foundation, and another is building on it. But each man must be careful how he builds on it. For no man can lay a foundation other than the one which is laid, which is Jesus Christ. Now if any man builds on the foundation with gold, silver, precious stones, wood, hay, straw, each man's work will become evident; for the day will show it because it is to be revealed with fire, and the fire itself will test the quality of each man's work. If any man's work which he has built on it remains, he will receive a reward. If any man's work is burned up, he will suffer loss; but he himself will be saved, yet so as through fire. (1 Cor. 3:10–15)

As believers, our souls rest on the foundation of Christ. Our works, however, will be weighed before what Paul called the *bema* seat. It's the same word used to identify where Gallio, Pilate, and Herod sat, and is sometimes translated "rostrum" or "tribunal." It is the place where a decision is made by the governing authority. In Paul's narrative, it is where only our works are judged, not our souls.

Paul also said, "For we must all appear before the judgment seat of Christ, so that each one may be recompensed for his deeds in the body, according to what he has done, whether good or bad" (2 Cor. 5:10). Again, the "judgment seat" is that *bema* seat. It is not the judgment Christ warned of (*krisis* in the Greek). The verb translated "recompensed" is not a payment for bad deeds. The Greek word means "to carry, bear, bring to." When our works are carried to the decision place of Christ, we will lose those "bad deeds" in the purifying fire of the Holy Spirit. That is a loss, but is it not a good loss? The only thing left will be "gold, silver, precious stones."

The idea of the *bema* seat frightened me for years—until I understood it. Now it gives me hope. I don't have to worry about the mistakes I've made. Like the dross removed from gold, my mistakes will be burned up and removed forever. Every outburst, every lie, every evil thing will be carried to his place of authority where he will separate the junk and burn it away. Only gold will remain.

My foundation is rock-solid. Nothing can move it. Now I can focus on "laying up treasures in heaven" through good deeds, which are those done in obedience to Christ, because the balance of my works will be purified and polished. For eternity, people won't see my dross. Just the gold!

Judge Not

There is one more aspect of judgment. It is the misapplication of the phrase "judge not." When taken as a commandment to never make a decision as to whether something is right or wrong in the sight of God, it exemplifies what happens when we don't understand context and fail to exercise discernment. The Greek phrase "*me krino hina me krino*" hinges on the conjunction *hina*. It connects the first "don't judge" to the next "don't judge." Essentially Jesus said, "Don't judge in such a way that you will escape judgment" (Matt. 7:1, author's paraphrase).

The Pharisees of Jesus' day served as judges and magistrates, deciding cases between the people and determining what was right and wrong. Instead of holding to God's standards, most were corrupt. They set their own standards and judged others accordingly. Therefore, when they cast judgment on someone, they made sure that they escaped the same judgment themselves. They judged in such a way that they could not be judged. This stood in contrast to the absolute, unchanging scales of the covenant law, which judged everyone by the same standards. But Jesus flipped that on them and told them that their merciless standards would be put back on them. His next sentence was, "For in the way you judge, you will be judged; and by your standard of measure, it will be measured to you" (Matt. 7:2).

Clearly man's judgment is not the standard by which God judges. He doesn't use any man's measure. Earlier in his ministry, Jesus spelled out the standards by which we should judge. He told the Jews in the temple at Jerusalem to "judge with righteous judgment" (John 7:24).

But what is righteous judgment? Righteous judgment is measured by God's Word and applies to everyone equally. When it comes to salvation, only God decides our case. In fact, he already has. If we are in Christ, we are clean. If we reject him, we are cut off and cast out. In other areas where we should exercise discernment regarding something or someone, we should do so according to his Word, not our own. When someone calls evil good, for example, he or she is setting aside what God has said and judging in such a way that his or her own evil deeds would not be judged. This is the kind of judging we are told to avoid. In whatever case we must make a decision, and we must do so righteously, which means according to God's standards.

Living the Promise

The promise of judgment is the assurance that Christ is our eternally secure foundation. We have been judged righteous in Christ. Upon him we can fearlessly build. So "let us hold fast the confession of our hope without wavering, for He who promised is faithful; and let us consider how to stimulate one another to love and good deeds" (Heb. 10:23–24). We are building something through our works, which will be weighed for eternity.

Don't fear mistakes; they will be removed, never to be seen again. Only that which is good will remain. When someone tells you that judgment is coming, you can smile as a believer and say, "I know. And I can't wait!"

CHAPTER 8

The Promise of the Kingdom

Your kingdom is an everlasting kingdom, and Your
dominion endures throughout all generations.

PSALM 145:13

Let's just get this out of the way now: I enjoy *The Walking Dead*. I know it's not for everyone. Zombies, gore, violence . . . it's messy. But there's an interesting side story in the later episodes with a group of survivors that call themselves The Kingdom. It's a little ridiculous. This colony uses phrases out of a King Arthur legend, even dressing up as if they're celebrating a perpetual Renaissance fair. Their so-called king sits on a wooden throne with a pet tiger on a chain. When someone from outside the colony presses him about the whole kingdom theme, accusing him of selling the people a fairy tale, he candidly says, "People want someone to follow . . . they want someone to make them feel safe."[1]

When Jesus arrived in Jerusalem, the Jews desperately wanted someone to make them feel safe. For centuries they had waited for someone to reestablish God's kingdom on earth. It had been promised throughout the ages and was briefly captured under King David. In fact, he wrote about God's everlasting kingdom as he sat upon the throne of his own kingdom, ruling over God's chosen people. But David's kingdom eventually fell.

Throughout history, people have looked for that kingdom of God to rise again and eternally. If his dominion was to endure throughout all generations, then surely he must establish his kingdom on earth, right? The Old Testament chronicles the rise and fall of the nation of Israel and God's kingdom of men. Even today, some Christians speak of a restoration of an earthly kingdom, complete with land, a city, and a throne.

But something radical happened when Christ proclaimed, "The kingdom of heaven is at hand" (Matt. 3:2). In fact, he was quite obsessed with this idea of a kingdom, considering how often he mentioned it. When we examine the idea in the Bible, we see something unexpected and glorious emerging from the shadows of the past. David's words were correct, but not necessarily in the way mankind anticipated. The result is a promise to believers today that if we will see the concept of a kingdom in the way Christ sees it, we can experience the benefits of occupying it.

Kingdom Defined

What exactly is a kingdom? The classic definition of a kingdom is "the territory subject to the rule of a king."[2] But there is another definition in the Greek word *basileia*, which is used in the phrase "the *kingdom* of heaven." It is a "royal power, kingship, and dominion not to be confused with an actual kingdom but rather the right or authority to rule over a kingdom."[3] In other words, a kingdom isn't necessarily a tract of land or a collection of cities. It is a sphere of influence under the authority of a sole ruler.

There's an AM radio station in Tallapoosa, Georgia, called WKNG. If you're in northwest Georgia, southeast Tennessee, or most of Alabama, you can tune in to this station for classic country during the daytime. Between Conway Twitty and Loretta Lynn, you might hear a voice declare, "You're in King Country!" Of course, the radio station doesn't own all of the land in that tristate territory, but its FCC license gives it the sole right to blast fifty thousand watts of power on a set frequency so that anyone who wants to listen can hear them. This sphere of influence is similar to the biblical concept of kingdom.

While the Bible clearly speaks of literal kingdoms, it also speaks of a WKNG type of dominion—one where anyone tuned in can hear it. Recognizing the difference between the two—physical and influential —enables us to live in "King Country," so to speak. Confusing literal and figurative kingdoms can cause us to miss the transmission. In the same way you can drive from Chattanooga to Atlanta and never hear a country song, you can walk through life and never see the kingdom of heaven, even though it's all around you. Such was the case with many people, including the religious Jews, when Jesus came broadcasting his message that the kingdom of heaven was at hand.

Expectations

Many of the Jews at Jesus' time expected a conquering king. They looked for one who would deliver Israel from Rome and restore Jerusalem to greatness. And why not?

From the time of Moses, they had been told, "You shall be to Me a kingdom of priests and a holy nation" (Ex. 19:6). God had promised King David, "I will raise up your descendant after you, who will come forth from you, and I will establish his kingdom. . . . Your house and your kingdom shall endure before Me forever; your throne shall be established forever" (2 Sam. 7:12, 16). When God promised restoration to Jeremiah, he'd said, "I will restore the fortunes of Judah and the fortunes of Israel and will rebuild them as they were at first" (Jer. 33:7). In exile, Daniel had declared, "His kingdom is an everlasting kingdom / And His dominion is from generation to generation" (Dan. 4:3). When Ezra was commissioned to rebuild the temple, King Cyrus proclaimed, "The LORD, the God of heaven, has given me all the kingdoms of the earth and He has appointed me to build Him a house in Jerusalem" (Ezra 1:2).

All they had known up until that point was a physical kingdom, a promised land with a throne in Jerusalem and a king to reign over them forever. From their perspective, a physical kingdom wasn't just the expectation, it was the promise. They no doubt knew the story of Ezekiel's vision in the Valley of Dry Bones:

> Then He said to me, "Son of man, these bones are the whole house of Israel; behold, they say, 'Our bones are dried up and our hope has perished. We are completely cut off.' Therefore prophesy and say to them, 'Thus says the Lord GOD, "Behold, I will open your graves and cause you to come up out of your graves, My people; and I will bring you into the land of Israel. Then you will know that I am the LORD, when I have opened your graves and caused you to come up out of your graves, My people. I will put My Spirit within you and you will come to life, and I will place you on your own land. Then you will know that I, the LORD, have spoken and done it," declares the LORD.'" (Ezek. 37:11–14)

In literal terms, this would be a promise of resurrection from the dead and a restoration of an earthly kingdom. At the time the prophecy was made, the Northern Kingdom lay in ruins; the Southern Kingdom had been conquered by the Babylonians. Nebuchadnezzar's chosen ruler sat on Jerusalem's throne, and the Jews that hadn't been exiled lived in virtual captivity. The promise of a restored kingdom would resonate strongly with the people. Ezekiel continued,

> Say to them, "Thus says the Lord GOD, 'Behold, I will take the sons of Israel from among the nations where they have gone, and I will gather them from every side and bring them into their own land; and I will make them one nation in the land, on the mountains of Israel; and one king will be king for all of them; and they will no longer be two nations and no longer be divided into two kingdoms. . . . And they will be My people, and I will be their God.
>
> "'My servant David will be king over them, and they will all have one shepherd; and they will walk in My ordinances and keep My statutes and observe them. They will live on the land that I gave to Jacob My servant, in which your fathers lived; and they will live on it, they, and their sons and their sons' sons, forever; and David My servant will be their prince forever. I will make a covenant of peace with them; it will be an everlasting covenant with them. And I will place them and multiply them, and will set My sanctuary in their midst forever.'" (Ezek. 37: 21–26)

There may have been a debate about whether King David himself would return to rule over the Jews, but there was agreement that the restored kingdom would be earthly and literal. This clear description of a perpetual kingdom, anticipated and expected, caused most Jews to miss Jesus, even though people did see that there was something special about him. Many recognized him as the "son of David," an allusion to the Old Testament prophecies that a king would come from David's descendants to rule forever. After he miraculously fed five thousand people, those present declared, "This is truly the Prophet who is to come into the world." They intended to take him by force and make him king, so he hid on the mountain (John 6:14–15). Upon his entrance into Jerusalem for the final time, they shouted, "Blessed is the coming kingdom of our father David" (Mark 11:10). All the while, many, including Jesus' disciples, operated under the assumption that Jesus had come to establish an eternal earthly kingdom and rescue Israel from its Roman rule.

When Jesus was brought before Pilate, just before his crucifixion, Pilate asked him if he was indeed the King of the Jews. "My kingdom is not of this world," Jesus told him. "If My kingdom were of this world, then My servants would be fighting so that I would not be handed over to the Jews; but as it is, My kingdom is not of this realm" (John 18:36). This statement was a game changer. In fact, this is the key to the promise of the kingdom. Looking for a physical, earthly domain with a throne made of gold and a king made of flesh and blood misses the kingdom of God. A literal view results in spiritual blindness. I can imagine a learned rabbi saying, "But I believe the Word of God!" He could then cite verse after verse proving that God's kingdom would be established in Israel, with Jerusalem as its capital. It's not an unreasonable position; it's just wrong. It caused Jesus' own disciples to question him at times. And it caused thousands, if not millions, to reject him when he didn't follow through on their expectations and instead pursued the kingdom of God in a way they could not understand.

The Kingdom According to Christ

Early in Christ's ministry, he was in Capernaum teaching in the synagogue, healing people, and casting out demons. People were impressed and tried to keep him from leaving, but Jesus said, "I must preach the kingdom of God to the other cities also, for I was sent for this purpose" (Luke 4:43).

I'd wager that if you went into any church and asked people what Jesus' purpose was, 99 percent would give you an answer other than "preach the kingdom of God." Their answers wouldn't necessarily be wrong, but if Jesus himself said that preaching the kingdom was his purpose, then the kingdom must be important. If it's important, then it might be a good idea for us to understand it properly.

Naturally, Jesus talked a lot about the kingdom. Matthew's gospel uses the phrase "kingdom of heaven." Other books, including parallel accounts in Mark and Luke, use "kingdom of God." There is no difference.[4] God doesn't have two kingdoms. Only humans come up with theological constructs that complicate, confuse, and conflate multiple kingdoms.

It's interesting to note how many times Jesus referred to God's kingdom in terms of physical, geographical territory, whether land, city, or region. The answer is exactly zero. He never spoke of his kingdom, God's kingdom, or the kingdom of heaven in measurable terms, like "from the mountains in the north to the desert in the south to the sea in the west." In the Old Testament people often spoke of physical places: Judah, Jerusalem, the promised land. They looked at physical things to validate their position or success: thrones, temples, cities, pastures. They did so because they lived in the shadows of what was to come. Their physical picture foreshadowed a spiritual reality.

John the Baptist directly addressed this paradigm shift when he said, "Repent, for the kingdom of heaven is at hand" (Matt. 3:2). The verb translated "repent" is *metanoeo* in the Greek. It doesn't mean "quit sinning" or "turn" or "confess" or anything we usually associate with it. Sure, those things often happen as a result of the original action, but they are not the actual meaning.

What we translate "repent" actually means "change your mind." John the Baptist was literally saying, "Change your mind, because God's dominion draws near." The verb translated "is at hand" is *eggizo*, an interesting word that is very often associated with the kingdom of God and New Testament prophecy. It's not an adjective meaning nearby, close, or here. It's a verb. It's an action. It means "to approach, to come near, or to join one thing to another." So John's message to the Jews, and ultimately to everyone, was that the dominion of God was actively approaching; and taking part in it would require a changing of minds about many things, including the concept of what a kingdom was.

Jesus began his adult ministry with the exact same message. After being tempted by Satan in the wilderness, he heard that John had been taken into custody. He went to Capernaum and "from that time Jesus began to preach and say, 'Repent, for the kingdom of heaven is at hand'" (Matt. 4:17).

As Jesus fulfilled his purpose teaching people about his kingdom, he often personified it. In several parables, he compared it to people: a farmer, a king, a landowner, and young girls. He twice compared it to a treasure. He also illustrated it with a net, a mustard seed, and the leaven in bread. Let's look at those last few examples first.

One theme of the kingdom is growth. The leaven in the flour, though a small percentage of the mixture, permeates and changes everything, causing the dough to rise and grow. The mustard seed, one of the smallest seeds, grows into one of the largest plants, reaching up to thirty feet in optimal climates. This is a picture of the spiritual reality taking hold in our lives when we receive Jesus' words. It grows into something we could never imagine when that small seed first germinates in our souls.

The idea of the kingdom as a treasure is obvious. Once you realize the value, you are willing to give up everything to obtain it. It takes spiritual eyes to see beyond the circumstances on the ground and perceive the riches just below the surface. The fact that so few do would indicate that people tend to miss his kingdom. But Jesus tells us that a vast spiritual wealth is ours if we will sell out to him and open our eyes to it.

The personification of the kingdom is more complex, revealing more detail. These illustrations, where Jesus likened the kingdom to people, assert the idea that judgment has a role in the kingdom's arrival. The well-known parable of the wheat and the tares provides a clear picture of this. Jesus said,

"The kingdom of heaven may be compared to a man who sowed good seed in his field. But while his men were sleeping, his enemy came and sowed tares among the wheat, and went away. But when the wheat sprouted and bore grain, then the tares became evident also. The slaves of the landowner came and said to him, 'Sir, did you not sow good seed in your field? How then does it have tares?' And he said to them, 'An enemy has done this!' The slaves said to him, 'Do you want us, then, to go and gather them up?' But he said, 'No; for while you are gathering up the tares, you may uproot the wheat with them. Allow both to grow together until the harvest; and in the time of the harvest I will say to the reapers, "First gather up the tares and bind them in bundles to burn them up; but gather the wheat into my barn."'" (Matt. 13:24–30)

In Matthew's account, Jesus then followed with the illustrations of the mustard seed and the leaven. But it was the wheat and tares that confounded his disciples, so they asked him what it meant. He explained it to them.

> "The one who sows the good seed is the Son of Man, and the field is the world; and as for the good seed, these are the sons of the kingdom; and the tares are the sons of the evil one; and the enemy who sowed them is the devil, and the harvest is the end of the age; and the reapers are angels. So just as the tares are gathered up and burned with fire, so shall it be at the end of the age. The Son of Man will send forth His angels, and they will gather out of His kingdom all stumbling blocks, and those who commit lawlessness, and will throw them into the furnace of fire; in that place there will be weeping and gnashing of teeth. Then the righteous will shine forth as the sun in the kingdom of their Father. He who has ears, let him hear." (Matt. 13:37–43)

Note that he said, "The kingdom of heaven may be compared to a man," then said that he was that man. When we ask, "What is the kingdom of heaven?" we might better ask, "Who is the kingdom of heaven?" It is Christ. To live in his kingdom is to abide in him. The words he spoke were seeds planted in the people of the world. Yet the world produces both sons of the kingdom and sons of the evil one. Jesus promised to send his angels to gather up both types of human crops and separate them. The evil ones would be destroyed, and the righteous ones would "shine forth as the sun," an allusion to Daniel 12:3.

Both Daniel and Jesus referred to an end, what some translations call the "consummation of the age."[5] The Greek denotes not the destruction of the world but the completion of an era. The arrival

162

of the kingdom of heaven signaled a new era, and those who did not receive Christ would receive judgment.

In his teachings about the kingdom, Jesus stressed the importance of hearing, understanding, and receiving his words. He was there to change people's minds about his kingdom. But when would they actually receive it? Would it be in their lifetimes, or was it still thousands of years away? Was it for this earth, or was it simply a picture of the afterlife? Where is your place in this kingdom?

Kingdom in the Epistles

Another clue to the expectations and parameters of the kingdom of heaven can be found by examining the letters written by Peter, Paul, John, and others, because these were written after Christ's ministry, crucifixion, resurrection, and ascension. Much debate has surrounded the meaning of "at hand," as in "the kingdom of heaven is at hand." Does it mean "near" or "here"? Personally, I don't think it matters that much to us now. If it didn't mean "here" during Christ's lifetime, then the nearness of it bears an inevitability of time. In other words, what was "near" but not "here" to the first century might be "here" today. Otherwise, it would not have been "near" to them. Fortunately, we can settle the debate simply by reading the Bible. Then we can see what it means to each of us today.

After the resurrection, Jesus appeared to the apostles and untold others. We don't know much about that period, but we do know that he spent forty days with his core group of disciples, presumably the remaining eleven after Judas Iscariot took his own life. What did he talk about? You guessed it: "things concerning the kingdom of God" (Acts 1:3). Kingdom was the strongest thread of his ministry on earth.

Still, the apostles expected an earthly kingdom. (I know it's really unfair, but in hindsight these guys seem really slow on the uptake!) "Lord, is it at this time You are restoring the kingdom to Israel?" they asked as he appeared among them (Acts 1:6). He sidestepped the issue by telling them not to worry about times and seasons. Then he said that power was coming through the Holy Spirit that would enable them to be his witnesses all over the earth. It's speculation, but I think they understood his words more clearly after Pentecost. The "near" fully became the "here" at that point. John the Baptist saw the dawn breaking, but those at Pentecost caught the full sunlight.

From then on, they almost exclusively spoke of the kingdom in the present tense. Only to Timothy did Paul reference a future entrance into the kingdom when he wrote, "The Lord will rescue me from every evil deed, and will bring me safely to His heavenly kingdom" (2 Tim. 4:18). Assuming that to be a reference to the afterlife is not really accurate, given his other references to the kingdom.

To the Romans, Paul wrote, "For the kingdom of God is not eating and drinking, but righteousness and peace and joy in the Holy Spirit" (Rom. 14:17). To the church in Corinth, he wrote, "For the kingdom of God does not consist in words but in power" (1 Cor. 4:20). To the Colossians, he said, "For He rescued us from the domain of darkness, and transferred us to the kingdom of His beloved Son" (Col. 1:13). He urged the Thessalonian church to "walk in a manner worthy of the God who calls you into His own kingdom and glory" (1 Thess. 2:12). For Paul, the kingdom of God was a contemporary reality. It was not future or distant. It was present and attainable.

Peter wrote, "Therefore, brethren, be all the more diligent to make certain about His calling and choosing you; for as long as you practice these things, you will never stumble; for in this way the entrance into the eternal kingdom of our Lord and Savior Jesus Christ will be abundantly supplied to you" (2 Peter 1:10–11). The door to the kingdom is open, but he leaves it up to us to walk through it.

The writer of Hebrews said that "we receive a kingdom which cannot be shaken" (12:28). Again, this is in the present tense. We don't await a kingdom; we receive it now. Even the book of Revelation, which speaks so much of events yet to happen at the time most of the canonized books were written, refers to the kingdom in the present. John introduced himself as "your brother and fellow partaker in the tribulation and kingdom and perseverance which are in Jesus" (Rev. 1:9). He partook in the tribulation and the kingdom, which would be impossible if it was not to come until thousands of years later. It had to be contemporary for him to take part in it.

The transition from the kingdom being "at hand" and "coming close," to the New Testament writers being "transferred to," "receiving," and "partaking" of that kingdom confirms that the kingdom of God came to earth. There is nothing to indicate it has ever been removed. In fact, the seventh angel in Revelation announced that once it came, it would stay: "The kingdom of the world has become the kingdom of our Lord and of His Christ; and He will reign forever and ever" (11:15).

If Jesus came to initiate his kingdom on earth, but we have to wait until life after death or some cataclysmic event to see it, then his work remains incomplete. But the scriptures tell another story. If there's any doubt left, just read what Jesus told his disciples about a week before he ascended into the sky: "I say to you truthfully, there are some of those standing here who will not taste death until they see the kingdom of God" (Luke 9:27). This is the definitive declaration that his kingdom would fully arrive soon. It was present wherever Christ went, and after he left, it would be present while some of the apostles still walked the earth. For us, that means it is here, now, in the power of the Holy Spirit.

The Promised Land

In the early part of the Old Testament, God repeatedly promised Abraham and his descendants a land to call their own. He described it as "a land flowing with milk and honey" (Lev. 20:24; Num. 14:8; Deut. 31:20; Josh. 5:6). He even said it would contain "great and splendid cities which you did not build" (Deut. 6:10).

The geographical location was in Canaan, which lies in modern-day Syria, Lebanon, Israel, Palestine, and Jordan (though its exact boundaries are disputed). It was intended to be a home for God's people—a place of security, prosperity, and an example to the rest of the world.

With the coming of Christ, the physical reality (which was merely a shadow of what God had in mind) elevated to a spiritual reality (which is the light). "Be sure that it is those who are of faith who are sons of Abraham," Paul wrote to the church in Galatia (Gal. 3:7). Here, he clearly stated that the descendants of Abraham were not related by blood but by faith in Christ. "If you belong to Christ," Paul wrote later in that passage, "then you are Abraham's descendants, heirs according to promise" (Gal. 3:29). Part of that promise was land. It is no longer a literal land but a place of spiritual security and prosperity that serves as an example to a world without faith.

The writer of Hebrews specifically addressed the promised land and "a city which has foundations" (11:10), meaning a physical location. He pointed out that most did not enter into and possess it, yet they still had faith to the day they died.

All these died in faith, without receiving the promises, but having seen them and having welcomed them from a distance, and having confessed that they were strangers and exiles on the earth.

For those who say such things make it clear that they are seeking a country of their own. And indeed if they had been thinking of that country from which they went out, they would have had opportunity to return. But as it is, they desire a better country, that is, a heavenly one. Therefore God is not ashamed to be called their God; for He has prepared a city for them. (Heb. 11:13–16)

This "better country" that is "a heavenly one" is the one Christ brought. It is a spiritual promised land where we abide in Christ and he in us. Just as the Israelites had to fight to possess their promised land, we must fight to possess ours. Yet "our struggle is not against flesh and blood, but against the rulers, against the powers, against the world forces of this darkness, against the spiritual forces of wickedness in the heavenly places" (Eph. 6:12). The heavenly places are promised by God to us, but spiritual forces of wickedness fight us. As the Israelites were guaranteed victory if they would engage in the battle in obedience to God, we have been guaranteed victory because Christ has already fought and won. We simply have to step into it.

A Holy City

In the Old Testament, God established his holy city in Jerusalem. "Blessed be the LORD from Zion," the psalmist wrote, "Who dwells in Jerusalem" (Ps. 135:21). There is no doubt that God chose that city as the center of his nation of Israelites. It was not only symbolic, but also literally the place where he manifested himself in the temple. There's also no doubt that those days are long gone.

"Speak to the men of Judah," God told Jeremiah, "and against the inhabitants of Jerusalem saying, 'Thus says the LORD, "Behold,

I am fashioning calamity against you and devising a plan against you"'" (Jer. 18:11). The prophet later called Jerusalem "desolate" and "a waste" (Jer. 33:10). Isaiah called it a "wilderness" and "desolation" (Isa. 64:10). The writer of Lamentations called it "an unclean thing" (Lam. 1:17). Zephaniah called it a rebellious, defiled, tyrannical city (Zeph. 3:1). Yet God still had plans for that city. As promised, he restored it and the temple. He sent his Son on a triumphal entry into the city for Passover. Then the people crucified him.

Jesus had acknowledged Jerusalem as "the city of the great King" (Matt. 5:35). Near the end of his earthly life, he wept over the city, saying, "Jerusalem, Jerusalem, who kills the prophets and stones those who are sent to her! How often I wanted to gather your children together, the way a hen gathers her chicks under her wings, and you were unwilling. Behold, your house is being left to you desolate!" (Matt. 23:37–38). He then foretold its doom, including the destruction of the temple, as we discussed previously.

When the city did eventually fall to the Romans, about a million people died and thousands more were enslaved. Where were the Christians during all of this? Most had fled, heeding the warnings of Christ and the writings of Peter and Paul. The Jews noticed their absence, and after this Christians were not permitted in synagogues.[6]

But the writer of Hebrews had told the Jewish converts, "We have an altar from which those who serve the tabernacle have no right to eat" (Heb. 13:10, 14). He went on to say, "For here we do not have a lasting city, but we are seeking the city which is to come." This New Jerusalem was a spiritual city where God now resided. John described his vision of it:

> Then I saw a new heaven and a new earth; for the first heaven and
> the first earth passed away, and there is no longer any sea. And I

saw the holy city, new Jerusalem, coming down out of heaven from God, made ready as a bride adorned for her husband. And I heard a loud voice from the throne, saying, "Behold, the tabernacle of God is among men, and He will dwell among them, and they shall be His people, and God Himself will be among them, and He will wipe away every tear from their eyes; and there will no longer be any death; there will no longer be any mourning, or crying, or pain; the first things have passed away." (Rev. 21:1–4)

At the close of the Old Testament age, the gospel of the promised Messiah had been preached throughout the Jewish territories. The prophecies of the prophets and Christ had come to fruition. The first earthly Jerusalem was no longer the holy city of God, and Christ's bride, the church, had a new location in a new heaven and earth where God dwelled. The old covenant, once fulfilled, became obsolete as the new one remained.

Paul likened the old and new to the mothers of two of Abraham's sons, Isaac and Ishmael. Ishmael's mother, Hagar, was a slave. Isaac's mother, Sarah, was free. "Now this Hagar is Mount Sinai in Arabia and corresponds to the present Jerusalem, for she is in slavery with her children," Paul wrote. "But the Jerusalem above is free; she is our mother" (Gal. 4:25–26).

The city is an important part of the kingdom. But like the kingdom Christ brought to earth, the city is not of this realm. The writer of Revelation saw a vision of "the holy city, new Jerusalem, coming down out of heaven from God, made ready as a bride adorned for her husband." We know who the "bride" is, figuratively speaking. It is the New Testament church. John further noted that "only those whose names are written in the Lamb's book of life" can enter this figurative city (Rev. 21:27). As the old, earthly Jerusalem was the place where

God's temple stood, the new, spiritual Jerusalem is where God now makes his temple, which is in the hearts of believers.

Peter had written of the coming "inheritance which is imperishable and undefiled and will not fade away, reserved in heaven for you, who are protected by the power of God through faith for a salvation ready to be revealed in the last time" (1 Peter 1:4–5). The readers of that letter received their inheritance, being spared from the destruction of the earthly Jerusalem by heeding Christ's warnings to flee the city when they heard rumors of war. The earthly kingdoms fell, and the spiritual kingdom arose. It continues to rise today, inviting you to live in it as it lives in you.

Seeing the Kingdom

Since we have established through Scripture that God's kingdom is now purely spiritual, how does that impact the way we engage with the physical? I believe it is hellish deception to think that because we are spiritual, we should not care about nonspiritual things such as politics, culture, science, education, and myriad other aspects of this life. Instead of disengaging with the world, those of us who have experienced a spiritual birth should engage the world to bring his kingdom into every arena. We are here to share his truth and love with a lost world. Hell tries to gate off its territory, but we are to storm those gates with the guarantee that we will prevail.

As we discussed, at one point Jesus sent seventy of his disciples out to testify about him, telling them to declare, "The kingdom of God has come near to you" (Luke 10:9). This is that same verb *eggizo*, meaning his kingdom has joined them. It's a little like that station ID: "You're listening to WKNG . . . King Country!" When we testify about the kingdom, we tell people the truth, identify its origin, and sow the good seed. We join every aspect of life with God's kingdom.

In that same passage, Jesus also mentioned what to do when people aren't tuned in. He basically said to keep moving because his judgment would come upon them: "The one who listens to you listens to Me, and the one who rejects you rejects Me; and he who rejects Me rejects the One who sent Me" (Luke 10:16). There was an element of the times in that passage, because the Jews were seeing the fulfillment of prophecy, which included judgment for those who rejected the Messiah. Still, the principle remains that we sow his Word in obedience, knowing that some wheat will grow among the tares. We are witnesses, not jailors or judges. We don't save people; God does. We point the way. Those who reject it continue growing "tares" as sin destroys their lives.

Another instructive point comes from Paul's assertion that "the kingdom of God does not consist in words but in power" (1 Cor. 4:20). The proof of his kingdom doesn't come on Sunday morning when the congregation is watching. It comes during the week when you're alone. It's not about how loudly it's declared, but how soundly it's lived. It's easy to make a show of it through forceful words, but the real measure comes in the daily grind. When transgression takes hold, discord sets in, discontent reigns, patience evaporates, and every other fruit of the Spirit withers; the kingdom of heaven is not present. Even so, it is near. It's just a matter of changing or renewing our minds every single day.

The way we live our lives indicates whether we are abiding in his kingdom. Paul encouraged believers to "walk in a manner worthy of the God who calls you into His own kingdom and glory" (1 Thess. 2:12–13). He goes on to say that we do this by receiving his Word. This evidence that we have received it comes when it "performs its work" in us. Its work is changing our minds. When our minds change, aligning with his truth, it changes how we think, speak, and act. It changes how we see others, both those who are saved and those who are yet to be saved.

Finally, our lives should reflect the truth that his kingdom is permanent. Jesus established it, and no man or spirit can tear it down. Every other kingdom will fall, but his will last forever. It resides with those who have been saved by grace through faith in Jesus Christ, who said, "Unless one is born again he cannot see the kingdom of God" (John 3:3). It does not reside in America, Israel, or any other geopolitical realm. It is present with a believer in Mumbai or Madrid, but not with a nonbeliever in Toronto or Tel Aviv. Man must erect fences and borders as long as there is evil in the world. We must appoint leaders to serve society for a time. Cities will be built to provide housing and commerce, but all of them will eventually go away. Only one will stand.

This is not a call to abandon the temporary because of the eternal. Just the opposite. Those with an eternal view are far more suited to steward the temporary. The one who believes "the earth is the LORD's, and all it contains, / The world, and those who dwell in it" will treat his creation with the respect due a king's possessions (Ps. 24:1). We just understand that there is more than what we can touch, see, and hear. We build our lives on more than the earth on which we live; we build it on an unshakable foundation.

Out of this establishment comes an attitude of service. The idea that we serve God in order to obtain his kingdom, whether in this phase of life or the next, is backward. "Therefore, since we receive a kingdom which cannot be shaken," the Bible says, "let us show gratitude, by which we may offer to God an acceptable service with reverence and awe" (Heb. 12:28). Our service and attitude should derive from already possessing his kingdom in our lives. It's one thing to serve our King in the hope of obtaining entrance into his kingdom. It's quite another to enter his kingdom and then serve him. Which would you rather do?

Living the Promise

The promise of the kingdom, a place where God reigns over his people, is that it's here and it's for you. You need not die to enter into his kingdom. It's as simple and profound as, "Your kingdom come." It comes when "Your will be done, on earth as it is in heaven" (Matt. 6:10). It brings peace, joy, and righteousness. Seek first his kingdom, and you will learn to walk in it every day.

His kingdom in your life impacts those around you. It can be beautifully shocking to people, like a blind man who suddenly sees. The promise of power in the Holy Spirit means you can touch others with the supremacy of his kingdom, showing them the entrance. You can be the spark to light a fire.

Don't look for any other kingdom, even one taking his name for its own vain purposes. There is no holy city or holy land. His kingdom is in his people, not dirt or bricks. Instead, live out the words of Christ:

"You are the light of the world. A city set on a hill cannot be hidden; nor does anyone light a lamp and put it under a basket, but on the lampstand, and it gives light to all who are in the house. Let your light shine before men in such a way that they may see your good works, and glorify your Father who is in heaven." (Matt. 5:14–16)

CHAPTER 9

The Promise of the End

*"I am the Alpha and the Omega, the first
and the last, the beginning and the end."*

REVELATION 22:13

Hal Lindsey terrified me as a young boy. Not personally (I've never met him), but the movie adaptation of his book *The Late Great Planet Earth* had me convinced I'd never see the age of thirty. The Soviet Union was going to invade Israel, and then Armageddon would throw the world into a state reminiscent of the Forbidden Zone in *Planet of the Apes*, just with no apes.

By the time I successfully hit thirty, I had grown comfortably numb to years of end-times prophecies. The Soviet Union had dissolved. I had personally taken a hammer to a section of the Berlin Wall as it fell. I had been to China and met some wonderful Christians working to bring the gospel to that oppressed land. The Branch

Davidians had gone up in flames, and the only thing left behind from an end-times cult called Heaven's Gate were their Nikes. I had heard enough so-called prophecy to know that it changed as quickly as our world. So I became a panmillennialist and tuned out. (The joke there is that everything will "pan out" in the end. It's a white flag in the face of eschatological debate and biblical confusion.)

Through the years, whenever I read scriptures related to the end-times or heard sermons that touched on it, a few things always bothered me. First, the disciples all thought they lived in the end-times. Just read what they wrote. If it wasn't "upon" them, it was "near" or "at hand." How could they all be so wrong? And if they were wrong about that, what else were they wrong about? That's a road that only leads to unbelief and disillusion.

Second, the various versions of the future we adopt tend to paint God as being on a merciless, bloodthirsty vendetta. Some predictions say he will gather all the Jews in Israel just to wipe two-thirds of them out. Others foresee plagues that will make Egypt look like child's play. All predict global persecution and martyrdom for Christians. But the God I have grown to know is full of mercy, patience, love, and hope. Yes, he is just and hates evil, but Christ has overcome the world. Yes, he allows suffering and tragedy in this fallen world, but he is not the author of it. The idea that he is waiting to wipe us out, or allow it to happen on a wide scale, seems pessimistic, fatalistic, and contrary to his nature.

Finally, nobody seems to get the end-times right. Predictions come and go about what will happen or when things will come to pass, and the same predictors that get it wrong keep on predicting. This is nothing new. Historically there have long been apocalyptic predictions that have not come true. Some of the perpetrators are dismissed as frauds, while others just tweak their predictions to move them a little farther ahead. To resolve the issues of pop eschatology, we'd have to perform an endless search for the one person who gets everything right, and I have yet to find that person.

Eventually, I turned to the fullness of Scripture. Not one verse here and one there, but entire passages and books. Context seemed to be everything. Digging into the Greek and cross-referencing the original language led to enlightenment. Studying the history of eschatology, even with all of its disagreements, was informative. Prayer, conversation, and research all led me on a fulfilling journey. I still don't have all of the answers, but now I have far fewer questions. Passages that once confounded me now make sense. Through it all I found a wonderful promise—a promise associated with "the end."

The End of the Age

Perhaps no single phrase has shaped Christians' view of the future more than the disciples' question to Jesus after his prophecies on the Mount of Olives. They asked about the *sunteleia aion*. This was translated in the King James as "end of the world," which certainly sounds like the destruction of the planet. A couple of updated King James versions (AKJV, KJ21) as well as the New Living Translation, American Standard Version, English Revised Version, and others still use "end of the world." The New King James Version, New International Version, New American Standard Bible, and International Standard Version, use the phrase "end of the age," which is truer to the Greek word *aion*. But since *sunteleia* is not a termination, but a climax or completion, the phrase "consummation of the age" is far more accurate. This is used in more literal translations, including the Berean Literal Bible and Douay-Rheims Bible. Others translate it as "full end of the age," "close of the age," "completion of the age," and, perhaps most accurately of all, "consummation of the system of things."

Since the question is not "When will the world be terminated?" but "When will the era be completed?" the discussion changes drastically.

To better understand the consummation of the age, we look to Hebrews, where the writer contrasts the old and new covenants. In this portion, he discusses how the physical temple, which was passing away, foreshadowed the spiritual work of Christ:

> For Christ did not enter a holy place made with hands, a mere copy of the true one, but into heaven itself, now to appear in the presence of God for us; nor was it that He would offer Himself often, as the high priest enters the holy place year by year with blood that is not his own. Otherwise, He would have needed to suffer often since the foundation of the world; but now once at the *consummation of the ages* He has been manifested to put away sin by the sacrifice of Himself. And inasmuch as it is appointed for men to die once and after this comes judgment, so Christ also, having been offered once to bear the sins of many, will appear a second time for salvation without reference to sin, to those who eagerly await Him. (9:24–28, emphasis added)

Again we see the Greek phrase *sunteleia aion*, translated here as the "consummation of the ages." It squarely puts the time frame for that completion in the generation of the writer, specifically citing Christ's crucifixion, and throughout the time of the writing of the New Testament. Why was it not complete with Christ's crucifixion, resurrection, or ascension? Or perhaps with Pentecost? To answer that, we look to the words of Christ where he specifically used the phrase *sunteleia aion*.

As mentioned in the last chapter, Jesus' parable of the wheat and tares included an identifiable marker of the end, or the consummation of the age. A harvest, Jesus said, would take place in this time frame, which the writer of Hebrews said included the crucifixion. All this would happen during the current generation living at that time. But get this: Jesus didn't say the harvest would happen *at* the end of the age; he said it *is* the end of the age: "The harvest is the end of the age; and the reapers are angels" (Matt. 13:39). Really, the "end of the age" is not so much a time, but an event.

So what did Jesus say would happen at this *sunteleia aion* event? He started with himself, the sower of good seed. The world is his field. The good seeds are those who believe, and the tares or weeds are those who rejected him. They are "sons of the evil one," a label Jesus also put on the Jewish leaders who rejected him. At the end of the era, a harvest would take place. Angels would cull the tares and, as a farmer would do with weeds, burn them up. This is all metaphorical, of course, so what was Jesus talking about?

Clearly those who heard his words, believed, and acted on them are the "righteous ones" in this story. That fact is confirmed throughout the New Testament writings. But if the consummation of the age took place during the first century, as Hebrews states, who were the tares that were gathered out of his kingdom and destroyed?

Jesus described them as "stumbling blocks" and "those who commit lawlessness." John later wrote, "Everyone who practices sin also practices lawlessness" (1 John 3:4), so there's a broad truth at play as well as a specific connotation. Who did Jesus target with this description? "Woe to you, scribes and Pharisees, hypocrites!" he said in his eight woes, which was an Old Testament–prophet type of judgment on the Jewish leaders who rejected him. "For you are like whitewashed tombs which on the outside appear beautiful, but inside they are full of dead men's bones and all uncleanness. So you, too, outwardly appear righteous to men, but inwardly you are full of hypocrisy and lawlessness" (Matt. 23:27–28).

He dropped a similar "woe" on those who stood in the way of those who came like children into the kingdom of God: "Woe to the world because of its stumbling blocks! For it is inevitable that stumbling blocks come; but woe to that man through whom the stumbling block comes!" (Matt. 18:7).

The end of the age could be viewed as the destruction of those who stood in the way of God's kingdom on earth in the hearts of men. The first stumbling blocks were the Jews who rejected Jesus and called for his crucifixion. Another identifiable stumbling block would be the Roman Empire that nailed Jesus to the cross and persecuted the early church. The majority of the Jews who rejected Christ were eventually gathered in Jerusalem and slaughtered by the Roman army in AD 70. The Roman Empire began its decline soon after. By AD 313, Constantine embraced Christianity, undermining the polytheistic, pagan foundation of the empire. It split into two empires, east and west, in AD 284, and by 476 it was gone. An empire that reigned for a thousand years, often terrorizing Christianity, was undone by it. The major stumbling blocks to God's kingdom on earth were removed as the age of Christ swept not just the world where Christ was born, but the entire planet.

The other place that Christ used the phrase *sunteleia aion* was at the Great Commission. The last words Matthew recorded recount a risen Christ appearing to his disciples on a mountain in Galilee. He gave them their final command, saying, "All authority has been given to Me in heaven and on earth. Go therefore and make disciples of all the nations, baptizing them in the name of the Father and the Son and the Holy Spirit, teaching them to observe all that I commanded you; and lo, I am with you always, even to the end of the age" (Matt. 28:18–20).

The literal translation of that last phrase is "See, I am present every day until the consummation of the age." We like to read that verse as if it were spoken to us, but the statement is more contemporary to his audience than we realize. Certainly, we have the promise of his presence in the Holy Spirit. But at the time, he was not only promising his presence for those he sent to spread the gospel, but promising an end of the era.

The End Is Here

If you've ever seen someone on the street with one of those signs proclaiming the end of the world and felt uncomfortable or embarrassed, your discernment radar was functioning properly. The destruction we should warn people of is the destruction sin brings in their lives, not some imminent calamity orchestrated by God. It is his will that none should perish but all would have eternal life. So when we read about the end in Scripture, we must understand the context.

There is a group of related Greek words used in the Bible that convey the idea of the end. They come from the root *tel-*, which originally meant a "turning point" or "hinge." The word we'll be focusing on is *telos*.

The noun *telos* refers to the termination, last in a series, ultimate purpose, or close of something. It does not refer specifically to the end of a period of time. Interestingly, it also means the payment of a toll or tax, and for those who rejected Christ, a heavy price was paid. The angel Gabriel used *telos* when announcing to Mary that she would give birth to Jesus when he said, "His kingdom will have no end"

(Luke 1:33). There is no limit to his kingdom or termination of it. It is everlasting.

Christ himself used this word when he said there would be wars and rumors of wars, but that would not signify the end (Matt. 24:6). A few verses later, he used it twice more, saying, "The one who endures to the end, he will be saved. This gospel of the kingdom shall be preached in the whole world as a testimony to all the nations, and then the end will come" (Matt. 24:13–14). He used *telos* when speaking of his role in Old Testament prophecy, saying, "For that which refers to Me has its fulfillment" (Luke 22:37). This is an enlightening use of the word. If we think of the end not as an expiration of time but as a fulfillment of a purpose, as the Greek word implies, then his predictions of the end are a completion of something and not the termination of the world.

The "gospel of the kingdom," the topic he called his purpose, would be preached to "all the nations" (which was, to the Jewish people, an obvious reference to the twelve tribes of Israel), and then the fulfillment would come. This raises the question, the fulfillment of what?

To understand this, consider the context in which this conversation took place. This was what's known as the Olivet Discourse, which simply means it's what Jesus said to his disciples while they were hanging out at the Mount of Olives. They had just left the temple in Jerusalem where Jesus had excoriated the scribes and Pharisees. As they were leaving, the disciples had pointed out some of the temple buildings, because the second temple in Jerusalem was quite impressive and a source of pride for all Jews. That's when Jesus said it would all come down—"not one stone here will be left upon another" (Matt. 24:2). Then they walked east from the temple for less than a mile to the Mount of Olives, and, naturally curious, the disciples asked,

"When will these things happen, and what will be the sign of Your coming, and of the end of the age?" (Matt. 24:3). It was in response to this continuing discussion that Jesus launched into a long prediction of events to come, forming the basis for much of eschatology, which is the study of end-times, typically understood as the future destruction of the world.

It's interesting that Jesus didn't repeat the disciples' phrase *sunteleia aion*, but shifted to the word *telos*. Both words point to completion, not cessation. In choosing *telos*, Jesus focused on the purpose of the period rather than the end of the world. When his disciples asked when these things would occur, Jesus put the definitive timeline on all of his end-times predictions. "This generation will not pass away until all these things take place" (Matt. 24:34).

Much has been made of the phrase "this generation." It has been deemed to mean a period of almost two thousand years, or a reference to a race of people instead of a group of those living at the time, or a completely irrelevant utterance, or a dozen other things. But what if Jesus actually meant "this generation"? What if he answered his disciples' question plainly? One of the biggest objections to this straightforward interpretation is the fact that the world didn't end in their generation. We're still here. But when you consider the meaning of the word *telos* and the phrase *sunteleia aion*, you quit looking for the world to blow up and start looking for fulfillment.

But fulfillment of what? I believe it is the fulfillment of the Law and the Prophets, as well as Christ's prophecies. The Old Testament law was the "system of things," to use the literal translation. It was the covenantal means of man relating to God. It laid out God's conditions, expectations, and consequences—both blessings and curses. That system ended. The climax was the destruction of Jerusalem, including the temple. Throughout the Old Testament, God warned his people through the prophets that if they did not receive him, they would face judgment. That judgment appeared as an invading pagan army. When Jesus came, he issued the same warnings. His judgment appeared as the Roman army. The generation of Christ heard the truth and had ample time to respond before their case was decided.

Telos is consistent in meaning throughout the epistles. Paul used it when saying the outcome of sin is death, but the outcome of sanctification is eternal life (Rom. 6:21–22). It's the same word in his declaration that "Christ is the end of the law for righteousness to everyone who believes" (Rom. 10:4). He encouraged the Corinthian church as they anticipated "the revelation of our Lord Jesus Christ, who will also confirm you to the end, blameless in the day of our Lord Jesus Christ" (1 Cor. 1:7–8). Paul also put a timeline on it when he explained how the events of Moses related to the early church: "Now these things happened to them as an example, and they were written for our instruction, upon whom the ends of the ages have come" (1 Cor. 10:11). Paul clearly stated that his generation was experiencing what is translated as "the end of the age."

The writer of Hebrews, who spent much time explaining how the shadows of the old covenant played out in light of the new covenant, used the same word when he wrote, "Christ was faithful as a Son over his house, whose house we are, if we hold fast our confidence and the boast of our hope firm until the end" (3:6). A few verses later, he said, "For we have become partakers of Christ, if we hold fast the beginning of our assurance firm until the end" (Heb. 3:14). Again, the end was contemporary to the writer. It was not some hope for the future long after he died. The hope of becoming the house of Christ was something he held to, looking for a fulfillment of that promise in his time.

The end was near in the sense that the fulfillment of Christ's prophecy and purpose would happen in his generation. The writer of Hebrews promised his readers their faithfulness would be rewarded:

> For God is not unjust so as to forget your work and the love which you have shown toward His name, in having ministered and in still ministering to the saints. And we desire that each one of you show the same diligence so as to realize the full assurance of hope until the end, so that you will not be sluggish, but imitators of those who through faith and patience inherit the promises. (6:10–12)

First came the end; then came the promises. Their inheritance was coming soon as the age of Christ came into fullness and the age of the law passed into history.

Peter demonstrated agreement with his use of the term as well. He wrote to a scattered group of believers who were "distressed by various trials" (1 Peter 1:6). He said that, despite their suffering and temptation, they were "protected by the power of God through faith for a salvation ready to be revealed in the last time" (1 Peter 1:5). Here, Peter used the phrase *eschatos kairos*, which carries a contemporary connotation of the end of a season. This phrase emphasizes the quickness of the conclusion, the "due measure" of the "last in a temporal succession," to take the Greek literally. He imported the term *telos* a few sentences later, where he wrote, "Though you do not see Him now, but believe in Him, you greatly rejoice with joy inexpressible and full of glory, obtaining as the outcome of your faith the salvation of your souls" (1 Peter 1:8–9). Again, the end was the outcome or fulfillment. It was for those scattered by the turbulence of the times (most likely the persecution under Nero) who anticipated the coming fulfillment of Christ's work of salvation as the high point and completion of an era.

What would that look like? Peter addressed that as well. He first said that it was coming quickly. "The end of all things is near" (1 Peter 4:7). In Greek, it is *telos pas eggizo*, meaning "the fulfillment of everything approaches," not "the world is about to be destroyed." (If we were to take it as a prediction of the end of the world, would that not make Peter a false prophet since the world didn't end?) A few sentences later, Peter spelled it out plainly: "For it is time for judgment to begin with the household of God; and if it begins with us first, what will be the outcome for those who do not obey the gospel of God?" (1 Peter 4:17). Here, the same word *telos* is translated "outcome," further emphasizing the idea that it is a fulfillment of a purpose, not a termination of the world. As is consistent in both the Old Testament and the New, the fulfillment of Christ's purpose carried with it the judgment of the nations of Israel, which is what Peter meant by "the household of God."

This particular Greek word, followed through its use in the New Testament, describes an era spoken of by the prophets, fulfilled through Christ, and ending in judgment on the house of Israel. It was the definite end of an age, signifying a turning point, which means that those of us alive thousands of years later live in a decidedly different age than Moses and the prophets. This transformational shift occurred because of Christ and took place in the first century. For the writers of the New Testament, the end was near—as was a new beginning.

Where in the World?

More clarity about the end comes when we ask *where* this foretold event was to take place. When the Bible speaks of the *world*, the meaning varies depending on the context. "For God so loved the world" denotes all mankind (John 3:16). "Do not love the world" refers to a materialistic, godless way of thinking (1 John 2:15). "He was foreknown before the foundation of the world" covers all of creation (1 Peter 1:20). When a man named Agabus prophesied that there would "be a great famine all over the world" (Acts 11:28), he made a regional claim, which history records at the predicted time in Syria.

Similarly, the phrase *all the earth* typically has a regional or societal quality. When Caesar Augustus decreed "a census be taken of all the inhabited earth" (Luke 2:1), they were counting the populace under Roman dominion, not the Chinese and Native Americans. The Jewish high priest Ananias brought charges against Paul in front of the Roman governor, claiming Paul "stir[red] up dissension among all the Jews throughout the world" (Acts 24:5). Again, the reference is not to faraway places, but the Roman Empire.

The same word ties back to Jesus' prophecies of the end-times. When he foretold the destruction of Jerusalem, he said, "There will be signs in sun and moon and stars, and on the earth dismay among nations, in perplexity at the roaring of the sea and the waves, men fainting from fear and the expectation of the things which are coming upon the world" (Luke 21:25–26). The word there is not the global term, but the distinctly regional Greek word *oikoumene*—the same one used to define where the census was taken. It is the same in Jesus' declaration, "This gospel of the kingdom shall be preached in the whole world as a testimony to all the nations, and then the end will come" (Matt. 24:14). Again the "whole world" is regional.

Prophetic passages regarding the world tend to fall into two categories: those affecting a region and those applicable to the worldly system of thinking and living (as opposed to God's ways). The end that Christ and most of the New Testament writers predicted has little, if anything, to do with some future destruction of the universe, but everything to do with the end of the era impacting the world in which they lived. As the promised Messiah fulfilled the covenant between the Israelites and God, their whole world changed. The new covenant those first Jewish converts preached to the Gentiles conveyed a wider message of salvation that truly went global.

Heaven and Earth

Another passage that once frightened me about the end-times relates to the predicted destruction not only of earth but of heaven itself. The same heaven where God lives and Jesus now sits (Matt. 6:9; Heb. 8:1), the one in which our citizenship resides (Phil. 3:20), and the one where we are storing up treasures to obtain an imperishable inheritance (Matt. 6:20; 1 Peter 1:4), is, according to some, supposed to be destroyed in a massive fire one day. How we could store up treasure that would not perish in a place that would perish and how the place where God and Jesus reside could burn up and be destroyed were things I could never reconcile. But Peter's words seemed to be pretty clear, especially in the context of a future end of the world.

> But the day of the Lord will come like a thief, in which the heavens will pass away with a roar and the elements will be destroyed with intense heat, and the earth and its works will be burned up.
>
> Since all these things are to be destroyed in this way, what sort of people ought you to be in holy conduct and godliness, looking for and hastening the coming of the day of God, because of which the heavens will be destroyed by burning, and the elements will melt with intense heat! (2 Peter 3:10–12)

Right in the middle of Peter's terrifying prediction of the destruction of everything, there's that question: What sort of people ought you to be? The implied threat in the face of complete annihilation should terrify everyone . . . until you understand what Peter was talking about.

Let's start with the word *elements*, which is a bit odd in the English. Is he talking about the periodic table? Everything from oxygen and helium to titanium and gold going up in flames? Maybe earth, wind, fire, and water? The Greek word is *stoicheion*, derived from a word that refers to an order of things. It's a word used to describe the organized way that soldiers march in formation. It means "a first thing from which others are derived." It relates to the letters of the alphabet as the elements of speech. It can indicate the fundamental principles of any art, science, or discipline. In a sense, it is related to the periodic table, in that something like water is fundamentally a structured order of hydrogen and oxygen, just as the word *book* is formed from the letters *B*, *O*, and *K*. But the focus in Peter's statement is the order, not the raw material.

Paul addressed this concept several times. In discussing his Jewish roots with other Christians, he said, "So also we, while we were children, were held in bondage under the elemental things of the world" (Gal. 4:3). A few sentences later, he pushed back against those who were advocating a return to the old-covenant law, saying, "But now that you have come to know God, or rather to be known by God, how is it that you turn back again to the weak and worthless elemental things, to which you desire to be enslaved all over again?" (Gal. 4:9).

To the Colossians, he also addressed this tendency to return to the law: "See to it that no one takes you captive through philosophy and empty deception, according to the tradition of men, according to the elementary principles of the world, rather than according to

Christ" (Col. 2:8). Then he asked, "If you have died with Christ to the elementary principles of the world, why, as if you were living in the world, do you submit yourself to decrees, such as, 'Do not handle, do not taste, do not touch!'" (Col. 2:20–21).

The *elements* both Peter and Paul talked about are the first principles, the underlying foundation of our faith, the parts that came before. Paul was referring to the Jewish law. Christianity is not an abolition of the law, as Christ pointed out, but a fulfillment. Yet with a new covenant, the first is made obsolete and "whatever is becoming obsolete and growing old is ready to disappear" (Heb. 8:13). If Peter and Paul are in agreement (and they are), we see that the elements mentioned by both are in context of the law of the old covenant.

These elements are directly related to the "earth and its works." The word for "earth" Peter used in this passage refers to the inhabited land. Its "works" are its deeds or undertakings. The phrase "the earth and its works will be burned up" readily identifies the accomplishments of mankind, as opposed to the business of God, and the fate of temporal things. Peter was talking about Christ's purifying fire coming to the hearts of men and the passing of the old covenant for a new and better one.

But what about the heavens? Surely Peter was saying that God's home (and our future home) will be destroyed by fire, wasn't he? The word for "heaven" is indeed the same Greek word, *ouranos*, that describes the residence of God. So is it, was it, or will it be destroyed?

In verse 10, the phrase "the heavens will pass away" is two words: *ouranos parerchomai*. *Ouranos* is, as we said, "heaven," which is properly defined as the sky, the things not of earth, the universe, or the residence of God. It's the same word in the Lord's Prayer that is part of the phrase "on earth as it is in heaven." The verb *parerchomai* literally means "to pass by, come near, arrive, or move forward." It is only used metaphorically to mean "pass away" or perish. And when Peter said that "the heavens will pass away with a roar," the word translated "roar" refers to a "loud noise" that grabs our attention. Altogether, this verse speaks of the kingdom of God coming near in a way that demands our attention.

But then there's the heat and the fire—an image that is more vivid and tending toward destruction, it would seem. The "burning up" of the earth and its works is the Greek word *katakaio*, which means "to consume by fire." It's the same word used in the parable of the wheat and tares when Christ would "burn up" the chaff at the consummation of the age. A couple of verses later it repeats the idea, applying it not just to the arena of man, but taking it to God's house by saying, "the heavens will be destroyed by burning." This phrase is three Greek words: *ouranos luo puroo*. Again, "heaven" is as we typically think of it. Then comes *luo*, which is a verb meaning "to loosen," as in the loosening of prison chains, a marriage contract, or a legal arrangement. It means the dissolution or annulment of something. It also applies to authority, when something is declared unlawful or no longer legally binding. The only type of destruction is the idea of destroying a compact, which is exactly what Christ did in making the law obsolete. If we take it at its core meaning, we don't see heaven being wiped out, but rather freed from the legal bonds of the old restraints. Again, this is precisely what Christ did. The way in which he would free the heavens of the law is described with images of fire. Finally, the word *puroo* speaks of being melted by fire and purged of dross. John the Baptist baptized with water, but said another would come who would baptize with fire. In fact, he used the same word, just the noun form, *pur*.

The purifying work of Christ promised to end the old system— that which was initiated by the Mosaic covenant. That legal foundation was purged on the cross, and a new foundation of grace was established, with Christ as the cornerstone. God's kingdom, through Christ, came near to man, heaven was freed from the requirements of the law as he satisfied it completely, and a new beginning for mankind was initiated. When we are born again (spiritually, not literally), we are "a new creation" (spiritually, not literally). The verse continues, "The old has gone, the new is here!" (2 Cor. 5:17 NIV). This transformation of earth reflects the transformation of heaven through the work of Christ.

Jesus spoke of this when he addressed a group of skeptical Pharisees:

> "The Law and the Prophets were proclaimed until John; since that time the gospel of the kingdom of God has been preached, and everyone is forcing his way into it. But it is easier for heaven and earth to pass away than for one stroke of a letter of the Law to fail. Everyone who divorces his wife and marries another commits adultery, and he who marries one who is divorced from a husband commits adultery." (Luke 16:16–18)

If you've been in the church for long, you've probably heard both of those last two statements, but never together. "It is easier for heaven and earth to pass away than for one stroke of a letter of the Law to fail. Everyone who divorces his wife and marries another commits adultery." Was Jesus ADHD, or did he put those two things together on purpose?

If you think his reference to heaven and earth passing away is a future prediction of the end of the world, then the following bit about divorce makes no sense at all. It's a non sequitur. But when you understand that heaven and earth passing away speaks of the end of the law as covenant, then the meaning starts to become clear. Jesus said that the law was operative up until John the Baptist, the one who said, "Change your mind, because the kingdom of heaven approaches." The kingdom Jesus spoke about assimilated not only Jews who recognized his kingship, but also Gentiles. People from every background wanted in, but the law was an immovable barrier. It wouldn't fail. The easier solution, Christ was explaining, was to dissolve the legal authority that ruled men and bound heaven. The only way to dissolve it was to fulfill it, which only he could do. As long as the "husband" of the law lived, divorcing it would be as the sin of adultery. But, as the Pharisees knew, when the husband dies, the wife is free.

This idea culminates in Jesus' parable of the fig tree, which he told right after making predictions of "signs in the sun and moon and stars" and "the Son of Man coming in a cloud." To explain his prophecy, he gave this picture:

> "Behold the fig tree and all the trees; as soon as they put forth leaves, you see it and know for yourselves that summer is now near. So you also, when you see these things happening, recognize that the kingdom of God is near. Truly I say to you, this generation will not pass away until all things take place. Heaven and earth will pass away, but My words will not pass away." (Luke 21:29–33)

Again, understanding the meaning of the passing of heaven and earth, we comprehend the prophetic utterances of Christ. It also fits the timeline of "this generation," since the physical manifestation of his prophecy was witnessed in the destruction of the second temple in AD 70. The fulfillment of his prophecies completed the turn from the age of the law to the next, under which we now live. It has been deemed the church age, the messianic age, the age of Christ, the age of grace, and a few similar things, but the label doesn't matter. What matters is that we understand that Christ's work was completed long ago. Of course, it's still ongoing as people pass through this life, but the end that he spoke of and the disciples wrote about occurred shortly after the New Testament was finished. Excerpting passages and changing their meaning to try to fit our future misses the glorious work of Christ and creates unnecessary fear.

Living the Promise

The promise of the end is the promise of a new beginning. It was the beginning of God's kingdom on earth in the hearts of men. It was the beginning of salvation by grace through faith. It was the end of the law, which only brings death, and the beginning of new possibilities in Christ. If you are apathetic, fearful, or pessimistic about the future, as I once was, it's time to change your mind. We're not here to await the destruction of his creation, but the implementation of his kingdom on earth in the hearts of men.

Christ brought his kingdom to earth so you could live in it and spread it. Rather than scaring people or turning them off with the message "the end is near," embrace and exude the hope that "the kingdom of heaven is here." Jesus promised a new era of hope, grace, power, and joy, not a future of death, destruction, and fear. That promised age is here. Walk in that light, and let his light shine in your world.

CHAPTER 10

The Promise of Eternity

*"Everyone who lives and believes
in Me will never die."*
JOHN 11:26

Eternity is a long time. Beyond our ability to comprehend, really. The ideas of resurrection and eternal life seem distant and almost fanciful. We live, we die, we lose loved ones, we quote Bible verses for comfort, and we often question our faith or even God. We hold to the hope of a future in heaven, but we carry the burdens of time and loss on this earth.

James called this life "a vapor that appears for a little while and then vanishes away" (James 4:14). The older I get, the more it feels that way. I have a theory about this. When I was fifteen, anxious to reach that age when I could drive, the thought of waiting another year felt excruciating. One more year amounted to an additional 7 percent of my life. Given that I don't remember much before I was about five, it felt more like 10 percent of my life. As I approach fifty, another year comprises closer to 2 percent of my life. Each year feels faster, because my perspective on life continuously evolves. Time is consistent; we change.

In order to view life, death, and eternity properly, our perspectives need to change. Spiritual maturity enables us to see beyond our years. Only then can we discover something closer to God's perspective. When we do, a startling truth presents itself.

In thinking of eternity, we typically place it after death. We live, we die, eternity begins. But what if I told you that you need not wait for eternity? What if it wasn't something strictly for the future, but for now? In the promise of eternity, there's a life-altering truth. One designed for you today. In fact, if you're not living in it, you're missing out on all that God offers.

Death

Death sucks. It hurts to lose someone. The shock or injustice of someone's sudden demise can be devastating. The suffering that often precedes the end changes both the victim and the loved ones who feebly try to cope with it. We are taught that someone who dies without knowing Christ goes to hell forever. This feels harsh, especially in the face of grief, and I can see why some people gravitate toward the belief that God doesn't send anyone to hell, that everyone's individual spiritual paths can lead to him. But as appealing as universalism is, I cannot justify this view according to Scripture.

If there's any area I'm wrong in my theology, I hope this is it. The idea of eternal suffering, separation, or nothingness gives me no comfort. But I can't deny the truth I see in Scripture about this. If your eternity is not secure in Christ, drop everything and put your faith in him right now. The truth is, you're not just in eternal jeopardy, but you're living a zero life right now. Life doesn't begin until you know Christ, so there's nothing more important, exciting, and eye-opening than an intimate, personal relationship with the Creator of everything. Seriously, if you're not absolutely, 100 percent sure that you know Christ, stop reading and find a Bible in print or online. Start with the gospel of John; then read the book of Romans. You won't understand everything, but you'll understand enough. You can be "born again" (John 3:7).

Even for believers, though, death can still be a problem. I've sat through funerals and heard the Bible quotations: "To live is Christ and to die is gain" (Phil. 1:21). "Death, where is your victory? O death, where is your sting?" (1 Cor. 15:55). "Whether we live or die, we are the Lord's" (Rom. 14:8). "Everyone who lives and believes in Me will never die" (John 11:26). All great quotes and inspiring truths, but often hard to hear while grieving.

Then there's this humdinger: "Precious in the sight of the LORD / Is the death of His godly ones" (Ps. 116:15). I mean, seriously . . . the psalmist makes it sound like death is a good thing! If you want to get all Hebrew on that word *precious*, you'll find out it means "splendid," "glorious," and "highly valued." Try responding with "Splendid!" next time you learn of someone's death. It won't go over well.

What is going on with God's view of death? Clearly, he doesn't see things the way we do. And maybe that's the problem (*our* problem, not his). Believe me, I get it. I've lost loved ones, and not just those who lived long, productive lives. I'm talking about those we lose way too soon. Prior to the service of my younger sister's funeral, the family walked through the auditorium. A relative on her husband's side looked at the massive display of flowers around the casket and said, "It's beautiful, isn't it?"

Without really thinking, I replied, "It's the ugliest thing I've ever seen."

It's brutal losing someone you love. God gives us some wonderful people, then seems to take them for no good reason. In the pain of such loss, remember this: God understands. Truly, he does. He's not some cold celestial absentee parent. The shortest verse in the Bible demonstrates it: "Jesus wept" (John 11:35). Here's the curious part: he wept over the death of Lazarus just before he raised him from the dead! Honestly, if it were me, I'd be stifling a smile. If I went to a funeral knowing I would walk up to the casket and say, "Get up!" and he or she actually *would*, I wouldn't be crying. I'd be thinking, *I can't wait to see the looks on their faces!*

So why did Jesus weep? Because he understood the pain of death in the hearts of humans. He felt it. There is no pain we can experience that he does not completely get. That's why I feel no shame shedding a tear over loss. My head knows one thing, but my heart feels another. And Jesus understands. He wept too.

The best way to prepare for the loss that death brings is to understand it when we're not grieving. I've had to work through this, and if you haven't already, you will. In my studies, I discovered three valuable truths that should change the way we view death and help us when our hearts are torn.

First, death is necessary. The reality is that our bodies are mere traps for our souls. We are not just flesh and blood. Given how corrupt our bodies are, that's good news. Maybe you're *People* magazine's "Sexiest Person Alive," but I doubt it. If you're like me, battling the body is an ongoing, often painful experience. Disease, degeneration, weight, and myriad other struggles plague the human condition. If this is all we have, we're in sad shape. Fortunately, our spirits exist, and in Christ, they are far superior to our bodies. Perfect, in fact. Even in our struggles, Christ makes us perfect—not in body, but in spirit.

Death, then, is necessary to free the perfected spirit from the imperfect body. Paul used the same illustration Christ used to describe death: a seed being put in the ground in order to grow a plant or tree. He said we are "sown a perishable body" and "raised an imperishable body" (1 Cor. 15:42). Through the saving work of Christ, all believers are destined for an improved existence, but it requires shedding this mortal shell. This life is a limit to our destiny. This is our journey, but not our destination. The mere seed of our physical lives must die in order to allow something greater to grow.

Second, the death we should be more concerned about is spiritual death. When John the Baptist was born, his father Zacharias prophesied over him and his role as a forerunner of the Messiah. Speaking of Christ, he echoed the words of Isaiah, saying he would "shine upon those who sit in darkness and the shadow of death" (Luke 1:79; Isa. 9:2). All those who lived under the law, Paul told us in the book of Romans, lived in the shadow of death because of the sin of Adam. Christ not only fulfilled the law, but he also broke the power of death, spiritually speaking, over all of mankind. For those who enter into life in Christ, death is conquered. But it is not a future victory; it is a present reality, "for the law of the Spirit of life in Christ Jesus has set you free from the law of sin and of death" (Rom. 8:2).

There is debate about the nature and timing of the resurrection of believers. Will it be physical? If so, when? What does a "perfected" or "glorified" body look like? Paul went into detail about it in 1 Corinthians 15, but there are still varying opinions among theologians. That's fine; we'll find out soon enough, and however it works will be better than we can imagine. The critical points are that (1) there is a resurrection, and (2) we can experience it, or at least the important part of it, right now.

The resurrection we experience now is spiritual. When Adam and Eve sinned, they died spiritually. Everyone since has been born with a sinful nature, so that requires a spiritual death of the old nature. We spiritually die in order to be spiritually raised. It's like what many churches say during baptism: "Buried in Christ in baptism; raised to walk in newness of life." This comes directly from Paul, who said, "Therefore we have been buried with Him through baptism into death, so that as Christ was raised from the dead through the glory of the Father, so we too might walk in newness of life" (Rom. 6:4).

Paul continued,

> Now if we have died with Christ, we believe that we shall also live with Him, knowing that Christ, having been raised from the dead, is never to die again; death no longer is master over Him. For the death that He died, He died to sin once for all; but the life that He lives, He lives to God. Even so consider yourselves to be dead to sin, but alive to God in Christ Jesus. (Rom. 6:8–11)

Life in Christ is a resurrected life. Our sinful natures, destined for judgment and death, die when we are "born again." This is an act of faith in Christ, his power over sin and death, and his rule in and over our lives.

Once death is conquered in us through spiritual rebirth in Christ, physical death becomes something entirely different. For all of the effort mankind makes to avoid the completely unavoidable reality of physical death, we would be much wiser to avoid the completely avoidable reality of spiritual death.

The third point about physical death comes from this spiritual truth, which is that physical death is not permanent. In fact, it's a minor event in a major transition. The Bible often refers to death as "sleep." Jesus said Lazarus was asleep. When his disciples took him to mean the nightly sleep we all engage in, he spoke in terms they would understand: "Lazarus is dead" (John 11:14). I don't think he was toying with them the first time. I believe he fully viewed physical death as a type of sleep from which all believers awake.

Paul used the term when discussing resurrection. He said that when Christ appeared after his resurrection, "he appeared to more than five hundred brethren at one time, most of whom remain until now, but some have fallen asleep" (1 Cor. 15:6). He meant that most were still alive, but some had died. Yet they were not spiritually dead, just asleep. That's why Jesus could say, "If anyone keeps My word he will never see death" (John 8:51). Obviously, many believers have died, but it's better regarded as a type of sleep because it is not a spiritual death.

There is evidence of some sort of intermediary place under the old covenant. Sheol was sometimes regarded as the place where the wicked went to await judgment, with the godly going to Abraham's Bosom, a place of comfort; some think that Abraham's Bosom was also located in Sheol.[1] There is disagreement on the literality of these places, as well as whether the dead left these places after the work of Christ or remained for future action, but many doctrines refer to Sheol and Abraham's Bosom places as between death and an eternal destination.

Most would agree, as I do, that when believers die today, their souls go immediately to heaven with Christ. Despite some theological positions to the contrary, I can't find reason to believe that this "sleep" includes a spiritual delay, whether waiting in some suspended state or entering an intermediate place. At Christ's crucifixion, one thief on the cross begged, "Jesus, remember me when You come in

Your kingdom!" Jesus' response was, "Today you shall be with Me in Paradise" (Luke 23:42–43). Along the same lines, Paul contrasted his embodied state with that of God's presence, saying he was at home in the body versus at home with the Lord, as opposed to being in a third, transitional place. Regardless of various ideas and interpretations, one thing remains: God graciously takes care of his own. In that, there is great comfort.

Luke wrote about Christ's resurrection with a beautiful phrase: "God raised Him up again, putting an end to the agony of death, since it was impossible for Him to be held in its power" (Acts 2:24). The Greek word translated as "agony" is *odin*. It refers to birth pangs, that agony a woman experiences before bringing new life into the world. For the believer, death is still painful, but it's not the end; it's the beginning. We transition from the confines of this earthly existence to a vast world previously unknown. While still in this "womb" we call life, we only see shadows and glimpses, the way a child in the womb experiences some sound and touch and learns to recognize the voice of his or her mother and even father. Hopefully, though, this prepares us for what is coming. We can learn to hear our heavenly Father's voice enough in this lifetime so that when the birth-agony of death pushes us into the next world, we recognize him.

As our view of death begins to conform to God's view, we can better appreciate Jesus' framing of his own death. To his disciples, those closest to him on this earth, he said, "A little while, and you will no longer see Me; and again a little while, and you will see Me" (John 16:16). Obviously his circumstances were different. We don't hop out of our graves for a friendly chat, then ascend into the sky. But what he said applies to all who believe in him.

The last words I said to my younger sister before she died were "See you later." I intentionally spoke those words, knowing her cancer was aggressively trying to take her life. I hoped to see her again outside of the hospital and in better health, but I knew that if she moved on to be "at home with the Lord," then it would simply be a matter of time—a short time—until I saw her again. A little while, and I no longer saw her. And again in a little while, I will see her.

This is death for a follower of Christ. Painful birth into a better life. A short separation from loved ones. Going home to live in the presence of the Lord. Precious in the sight of God. Not so scary after all.

Resurrected Life

In the meantime, those of us here on earth battling the challenges of life can and should experience a taste of heaven. Spiritual resurrection is not meant to be insurance for the future. It is designed to radically impact the present.

When Jesus' friend Lazarus died, he went to Bethany to see the family. Lazarus's sister, Martha, said in her grief, "Lord, if You had been here, my brother would not have died." Jesus responded by saying, "Your brother will rise again." Familiar with the teachings on the resurrection (whether from the synagogue or from Christ we don't know), Martha said, "I know that he will rise again in the resurrection on the last day" (John 11:21–24).

Judaism has long divided the ages into three periods: the first, before the law; the second, under the law; the third, under the Messiah. The "last day" always referred to the messianic age. Given that the Messiah was standing right in front of her, it would be correct for Martha to say that she was living in the last day. Whether the messianic age began at Christ's birth, death, resurrection, or the judgment and fulfillment of his prophecies didn't really matter at that moment. He was there.

Martha exhibited a typical attitude regarding the resurrection, both for her time and for many people today. She viewed it as an event reserved for the distant future. It may give hope for later, but it provides little comfort for today. But when we focus on the *when* or *how*, we miss the truth of the resurrection. The issue is the *who*.

"I am the resurrection," Jesus said to Martha (John 11:25). She had faith for a future event in the form of a theological position; he offered hope for her immediate pain in the form of a tangible presence. Then, in a stunning illustration of his words, he raised her brother from the dead.

Lazarus's resurrection was just the beginning. When we look at specific occurrences of physical resurrection in the Bible, we see that in fact a mass transition of the dead happened after Christ's crucifixion. At the moment he died, the temple veil ripped in two and "the tombs were opened, and many bodies of the saints who had fallen asleep were raised; and coming out of the tombs after his resurrection they entered the holy city and appeared to many" (Matt. 27:52–53). This is likely a fulfillment of Hosea's statement, "He will revive us after two days; / He will raise us up on the third day, / That we may live before Him" (Hos. 6:2).

There is no historical corroboration of such an event, causing secular historians and some Bible scholars to reject its literality. But that shouldn't be much of a surprise, given that so many miss the messianic nature of Christ and reject his supernatural acts and claims of divinity. A blind man doesn't know if the light is on or off. Even the Jewish scholars of Jesus' lifetime split over the idea of a resurrection. The Pharisees believed in it, but the Sadducees did not, even though they all studied the same scrolls. But Paul vehemently argued in favor of such a thing: "If there is no resurrection of the dead, not even Christ has been raised; and if Christ has not been raised, then our preaching is vain, your faith also is vain" (1 Cor. 15:13–14). For the believer, there is a resurrection after death. Theologians split over whether it is immediate or delayed, strictly spiritual or also physical, but there should be no doubt that death is not the end. It's the beginning.

At the same time, there is another beginning, another resurrection that occurs prior to death. Eternal life enters us when we are "born again," as Christ explained to Nicodemus (John 3). Spiritually, our "old man" dies, and we are born into a new life. This is the resurrection we receive in the present. Lazarus was a physical illustration of a spiritual truth. We need not wait until we die to experience it.

Paul wrote,

> In Him you have been made complete . . . having been buried with Him in baptism, in which you were also raised up with Him through faith in the working of God, who raised Him from the dead. When you were dead in your transgressions and the uncircumcision of your flesh, He made you alive together with Him, having forgiven us all our transgressions, having canceled out the certificate of debt consisting of decrees against us, which was hostile to us; and He has taken it out of the way, having nailed it to the cross. (Col. 2:10, 12–14)

Here we see the concepts of completion and resurrection in the spiritual sense, contemporary in the lives of the first-century Christians. This removal of sin's penalty, which is death, was made possible at the cross. Its application is continuous throughout the messianic age, covering all of us today. The hope of a future physical resurrection is preceded by and inspired by the evidence of a present spiritual resurrection.

Eternal Life Now

Jesus upset a lot of people, especially religious experts, when he claimed to be the giver of eternal life. To the Jews of his day, he said,

> "Truly, truly, I say to you, he who believes has eternal life. I am the bread of life. Your fathers ate the manna in the wilderness, and they died. This is the bread which comes down out of heaven, so that one may eat of it and not die. I am the living bread that came down out of heaven; if anyone eats of this bread, he will live forever." (John 6:47–51)

Christ is the giver of eternal life. He doesn't ask us to wait for it. He invites us to partake of that divine meal even while living on this earth. Consider the exhortation of Paul to his fellow evangelist, Timothy: "Take hold of the eternal life to which you were called" (1 Tim. 6:12). He said this to a fellow believer, implying that one could have hope for a future eternity without presently embracing it. As one called by God, Timothy would experience eternal life eventually, but Paul urged him not to wait, to "take hold" of it now. One meaning of the original word is "to seize it." There is a purposeful aggression in Paul's word choice. As Timothy's mentor in the faith, he was unambiguously telling the young believer to demonstrate some boldness and intentionality regarding the eternal life already available to him. The same applies to us today. Eternal life awaits us, so we should reach out and grab it.

John alluded to this concept when he warned, "Everyone who hates his brother is a murderer; and you know that no murderer has eternal life abiding in him" (1 John 3:15). Was he suggesting that anyone who harbors hatred cannot go to heaven? No. We know that all can be forgiven if we ask. Was he saying that anyone who hates his brother is not a Christian? No. *Brother* is used figuratively and is not limited to blood relations. John was talking about one who hates his brother in Christ, or other Christians. John went on to say, "Whoever has the world's goods, and sees his brother in need and closes his heart against him, how does the love of God abide in him?" (1 John 3:17). Here he framed a parallel condition: a believer who does not act in obedience lacks all that God offers.

His assertions establish three things: First, a believer can harbor hatred, which is vile. Second, eternal life should "abide" in believers. *To abide* means "to continually be held in place, to remain, and to be present." Third, holding to ungodly attitudes can cause believers to miss out on the fullness of life that Christ intends for us. Frustrated or unfruitful Christians need to hear this. Aggressively pursuing a full life in Christ is an essential part of our calling.

So if eternal life is not just life after death, what is it? That would be a highly debated question if Jesus hadn't spelled it out himself. Just before Judas's betrayal, in what is often called the High Priestly Prayer, Jesus said to the Father, "This is eternal life, that they may know You, the only true God, and Jesus Christ whom You have sent" (John 17:3).

Eternal life is knowing God, the Eternal One. Can we know God now? Yes. Do we know him through Jesus Christ? Yes. Therefore, we can have eternal life now, but we must take hold of it.

To provide a rudimentary picture of this, imagine a young man courting a young girl. How does he go about "taking hold" of her in a proper way? He pursues her by looking for any excuse to be with her. He initiates conversations with her and then listens to whatever she says. He does things solely to please her—not because she demands it, but because he wants to. He thinks about her constantly. He gives no attention to other girls who come his way, no matter how attractive or aggressive they may be. When it comes to capturing her heart, he is fully committed.

The good news about eternal life through knowing God is that he's not a fickle teenage girl. In fact, he's more like the young man. He has given his absolute best so that we can know him. Our pursuit of him is less an exercise on our own part than an acceptance of his overtures. To use another analogy, he has set the banquet table and invites us to dine with him in fellowship now. If you are unsatisfied with your life or simply want to experience more, take your place at his table and get as much as you can. Follow the lead of the psalmist and "taste and see that the LORD is good" (Ps. 34:8).

Living the Promise

The promise of eternity is the guarantee that believers will live forever with God but also that we can taste eternity now. It changes our perspectives on death, which in turn changes our perspectives on this life. The small things of this life become even smaller in the long lens of eternity. The things important or impressive in this world seem insignificant and even silly compared to the things that will last forever.

An eternal view also inspires us to "lay up treasures in heaven." While the world builds sand castles, we can build a seaside mansion. Doing so becomes a joy. Being free of the pressure to invest in things that will not last removes the weighty burdens this world tries to impose. There is so much freedom in this promise that it's no wonder Christ spent so much time talking about it. He truly wants us to understand and embrace this truth. We are purposely designed to walk each day in the truth that the apostle John laid out: "We know that the Son of God has come, and has given us understanding so that we may know Him who is true; and we are in Him who is true, in His Son Jesus Christ. This is the true God and eternal life" (1 John 5:20).

This is a big promise, backed up by the Creator and Ruler of the universe. He came to earth as one of us to make all of these promises a reality. Still, he gives us the choice. God does not take hostages. He makes glorious promises and delivers when we follow his direction. Choose it. Believe it. Live it.

Conclusion

A New Beginning

As the age of the old covenant was fulfilled in Christ, he initiated a new covenant that no longer depends on mankind. The Israelites' failure to follow the law demonstrated human imperfection, repeatedly breaking the relationship between God and his people. But with Christ's perfection, the new covenant can never be broken because it is between the Father and the Son. All of mankind is now invited into a personal relationship with God by his grace and through our faith.

The promises we see in this new era of Christ's atonement and supremacy allow us to live lives of purpose and power as we build his spiritual kingdom on earth. The past teaches us about the present by providing a blueprint for expanding his influence. Christ's finished works facilitate a future free from fear, giving us the authority and confidence to act on his behalf.

Our mission is simple: partake in his victory and proclaim his lordship. Our works should reflect this truth. We are not striving to attain salvation; we receive it as a gift. We are not doomed to be defeated at the hands of the Enemy; he is conquered. We are not intended to wander in a spiritual desert; his promised land awaits our entrance now. Even so, there is still a fight, as there often was in the days of Israel.

As we proclaim and demonstrate these truths, we wield the spiritual weapons of love, mercy, humility, character, strength, and every other attribute of Christ. We are reborn to conquer every thought, attitude, and spirit that seeks to deny the kingdom of God. The enemy is defeated. He was overcome by the blood of Christ and the testimony of those who believed. Our testimonies affirm his victory for all who will believe. We can triumph because Christ has won. And that is a promise.

Acknowledgments

Special thanks to all of those who challenge and encourage
my efforts to understand and communicate the Gospel.
To my parents, James and Betty Robison, for
a lifetime of prayer and support.
To my wife and children, for putting up
with long days and late nights.
To everyone at LIFE Outreach International
for serving to share the love of Christ.
To Terry Redmon for wisdom, patience, and support.
To Dudley Hall for solid biblical and theological insight.
To Scott McDuffie for long conversations seeking truth.
To Randal Taylor for always believing and making things happen.

About the Author

Randy Robison is a writer, producer, and cohost for the television program *LIFE Today*. He also ghostwrites columns and books for his father, James Robison. He is a graduate of Oral Roberts University, a husband, and a father of four. He and his family make their home in the Dallas–Fort Worth area.

Notes

Chapter 1: The Promise of Deliverance

1. Joseph Thayer, *Thayer's Greek-English Lexicon of the New Testament*, 2nd ed., s.v. "ῥύομαι," (New York: American Book Company, 1889).

Chapter 2: The Promise of Sacrifice

1. *Qarab* is the Hebrew root. *The Brown-Driver-Briggs Hebrew and English Lexicon*, "Hebrew Lexicon entry for Qarab," (Peabody, MA: Hendrickson Publishers, 1902).
2. See Lev. 27, Num. 18, and Deut. 14.

Chapter 3: The Promise of the Law

1. *Thayer's Greek Lexicon*, s.v. "παιδαγωγός."
2. G. K. Chesterton, *St. Francis of Assisi* (New York: George H. Doran, 1924; Mineola, NY: Dover, 2012), 9. Citations refer to the Dover edition.
3. Title 11, Delaware Criminal Code § 1325A (June 2000).
4. New Hampshire Revised Statute § 207:48 (2015).

Chapter 4: The Promise of the Chosen People

1. This is supported in many places, including *Historia de los judíos argentinos* by Ricardo Feierstein (Buenos Aires: Galerna, 2006), 18.

2. Manasseh ben Israel, *The Hope of Israel* (London: R. I. for Hannah Allen, at the Crown in Popes-head Alley, 1650). Section 2, page 8: "They anciently were white men, bearded, and civil in converse." Section 37, page 43: "4. That at this day they keep the Jewish Religion. 5. That the prophecies concerning their return to their Country, are of necessity to be fulfilled."

3. *The Doctrine and Covenants of the Church of Jesus Christ of Latter-Day Saints Containing Revelations Given to Joseph Smith, the Prophet, with Some Additions by his Successors in the Presidency of the Church* (1839; Salt Lake City: Intellectual Reserve, 1981), 49:24.

4. Herbert W. Armstrong, *The United States and Britain in Prophecy* (Pasadena: Ambassador College Press, 1980), 147.

5. Gérard Lucotte and Pierre Smets, "Origins of Falasha Jews Studied by Haplotypes of the Y Chromosome," *Human Biology* 71, no. 6 (December 1999): 989–93.

6. Andrew Tobin, "Ashkenazi Jews Descend from 350 People, Study Finds," *Jewish Times*, September 10, 2014, http://www.timesofisrael.com /ashkenazi-jews-descend-from-350-people-study-finds/.

Chapter 5: The Promise of the Priest

1. Hebrew: *shachah*. Greek: *proskuneo*.
2. Hebrew: *'abad*. Greek: *latreia*.

Chapter 6: The Promise of the Temple

1. SORROWS, comment on "Are Protestant Churches Also 'the House of God,'" Catholic Answers, June 18, 2007, https://forums.catholic.com /t/are-protestant-churches-also-the-house-of-god/76597/7.

2. Josephus, *The Jewish War*, trans. William Whiston in *The Works of Flavius Josephus* (Cincinnati: E. Morgan, 1841), 5.10.5.

3. Ibid., 5.12.3.
4. Ibid., 5.11.1.
5. Ibid., 5.13.4.

Chapter 7: The Promise of Judgment

1. *Old Hebrew Lexicon—New American Standard*, s.v. "mishpat," Bible Study Tools, http://www.biblestudytools.com/lexicons/hebrew/nas

/mishpat.html. BibleStudyTools.com's Greek lexicon is based on *Thayer's Greek-English Lexicon of the New Testament* and *Smith's Bible Dictionary* plus others; this is keyed to the large Kittel and the *Theological Dictionary of the New Testament*.

Chapter 8: The Promise of the Kingdom

1. "The Well," *The Walking Dead*, season 7, episode 2, directed by Greg Nicotero, aired October 30, 2016 (New York: AMC Networks, 2016).
2. *A Greek-English Lexicon of the New Testament: Being Grimm's Wilke's Clavis Novi Testamenti* (n.p.: Harper & Brothers, 1892), s.v. "kingdom."
3. *New Testament Greek Lexicon—New American Standard*, s.v. "basileia," BibleStudyTools.com, http://www.biblestudytools.com/lexicons/greek /nas/basileia.html.
4. Cf. Matthew 13:31; Mark 4:30; Luke 13:18.
5. Cf. Matthew 13:39 in the Douay-Rheims Bible and the Berean Literal Bible.
6. "A. D. 70 Titus Destroys Jerusalem," *Christianity Today*, http://www .christianitytoday.com/history/issues/issue-28/ad-70-titus-destroys -jerusalem.html.

Chapter 10: The Promise of Eternity

1. Joe Rigney, "He Descended into Hell?" Desiring God, April 4, 2015, http://www.desiringgod.org/articles/he-descended-into-hell.